STUDENT AFFAIRS RECONSIDERED

A Christian View of the Profession and its Contexts

D1462095

Edited by

David S. Guthrie

Calvin Center Series
and
University Press of America, Inc.
Lanham • New York • Oxford

Copyright © 1997 by
University Press of America,® Inc.
4720 Boston Way
Lanham, Maryland 20706

12 Hid's Copse Rd.
Cummor Hill, Oxford OX2 9JJ

Copublished by arrangement with the Calvin Center for Christian
Scholarship

Library of Congress Cataloging-in-Publication Data

Student affairs reconsidered : a Christian view of the profession and its
contexts / edited by David S. Guthrie.
p.   cm.
Includes bibliographical references.
1. Student affairs services. 2. Church and college. I. Guthrie, David
S., 1956-.
LB2342.9.S78   1997   259'.24--dc21   97-17068 CIP

ISBN 0-7618-0794-2 (cloth: alk. ppr.)
ISBN 0-7618-0795-0 (pbk: alk. ppr.)

CONTENTS

Acknowledgments

SOME PEOPLE BELIEVE in you and some don't. Those that do often express their believing by helping you give voice to your ideas and visions. Ronald A. Wells, the Director of the Calvin Center for Christian Scholarship, is one of these believers. In an environment where it is uncommon if not undignified to mention student affairs and scholarship in the same breath, Dr. Wells believed in my colleagues and me. Over the last three years, his believing translated into constant support, tender reproof, and timely guidance. Most importantly, due to Dr. Wells believing and the subsequent support of the Calvin Center, a Christian voice, albeit a nascent one, is no longer conspicuously absent from the conversation.

Many thanks also go to Donna Romanowski, the amiable and able assistant in the Calvin Center. Donna contributed graciously to this project as she does many others: she was a constant source of enthusiasm and support for me as I completed editorial tasks. Many otherwise wearying days working on the project were redeemed and enriched because of her quick smile, contagious spirit, and common sense.

Finally, we acknowledge with gratitude the many people, experiences, educations, conversations, and books that stood behind our resolve to make this book a reality. In particular, we extend our deep appreciation to those loved ones with whom we live and to those colleagues with whom we work—because, more often than not, they believe in us most of all.

D. S. G.

Foreword

THIS BOOK IS a product of the Calvin Center for Christian Scholarship (CCCS), which was established at Calvin College in 1977. The purpose of the CCCS is to promote creative, articulate and rigorous Christian scholarship that addresses important theoretical and practical issues.

The present volume results from the ideas of Jeanette Bult De Jong and David S. Guthrie, the two main officers of the student life division at Calvin College. Their hope, both in forming a working group of student life scholars and in the book that would issue from their work, was to bring the theory and practice of student life into the discourse about higher education in North America. The group met over three years under the auspices and funding of the CCCS.

The main idea in this book is concerned with how, and what, students actually learn in college. Most honest academics now realize that "the curriculum" is not the only mode of learning, even as much as we now admit that the term "extra-curricular" perpetuates the old typology. Indeed, rather than speaking of the "co-curriculum" we now suggest it best to speak of the "whole curriculum." Therefore, from the viewpoint of religiously-based colleges that seek the development of the whole person, intellectuals of all disciplines should welcome the contributions of their colleagues in student life.

We at the CCCS are aware that this book is not the last word on the subject of developing a Christian perspective on student life. Indeed, conscious as we are that there has been little writing on the subject—that this is closer to the first word than the last—we are delighted to present this volume in the hope that it will give a strong voice to the growing discourse on bringing the theory and practice of student life fully into its academic and intellectual setting.

Grand Rapids   Ronald A. Wells
March, 1997   Director, CCCS

Introduction

David S. Guthrie

ALMOST FIVE YEARS ago, several people sat around a conference table at Calvin College in Grand Rapids, Michigan, to consider the possibility of forming a study group to examine the student affairs profession with a particular eye toward exploring it from a Christian point of view. Two particular concerns fueled our interest. On the one hand, we expressed disappointment regarding the seemingly uncritical ways in which many Christian student affairs professionals understand and enact their work. We were chagrined that Riggs' critique of more than thirty years ago still seemed to ring true: "Perhaps we have been so concerned with establishing educationally acceptable techniques and policies in personnel work that we have not thought of them in their Christian perspectives" (1962, p. 15). Ultimately, we wanted to believe that a Christian student affairs professional was more than an odd hybrid of chaplain and campus security officer who mimicked contemporary theory and practice—or ignored it altogether.

On the other hand, we were concerned about the state of the student affairs profession in general. We were painfully aware of those who were writing that the field is unclear about what to call itself (Bucci, 1993) and that the profession lacks "consensus concerning [its] purposes and roles" (Whitt, Carnaghi, Matkin, Scalese-Love, & Nestor, 1990, p. 179). Stamatakos and Rogers (1984, pp. 400, 410) were particularly disturbing to us:

> The profession of college student affairs is in a state of confusion, discordance, and doubt about its appropriate role in a changing collegiate environment . . .The profession not only lacks a coherent and consistent philosophy but also lacks understanding and agreement regarding the individual components that constitute such a philosophy . . .Without knowing what it believes, its values have no grounding other than rerooting themselves in the expediency of what the profession does.

The conversations of that November day, in fact, resulted in the formation of a study group and subsequently to the funding of our efforts by the Calvin Center for Christian Scholarship and the writing of this book. It is fair to say that our initial zeal and optimism about the task waxed and waned from time to time. It also became obvious that it was impossible to discuss the student affairs profession outside of the context of higher education in general. As a result, our conversations often drifted to much larger contexts of academe including teaching, accreditation, curriculum, secularization, and the like. Working through the issues as a group—our personal beliefs and ecclesiastical traditions, our perceptions about "what's going on" in the field, what material to include and what to omit, whether a particular approach reflected a Christian view, when it was time to "move on," and so on—was not always easy, and conversations were never finished. In the final analysis, perhaps that is as it should be—or, must be.

Perhaps the issue with which we wrestled most was the appropriate "voice" of the book. We began the project with a desire to generate conversations among our Christian student affairs colleagues—many of whom work at Christian colleges—around questions such as: What may differentiate a Christian student affairs professional from colleagues who do not adhere to Christian faith? What are the contours of Christian faithfulness in pursuing one's calling as a student affairs professional (Thomas, 1992)?

As time went on, however, we sensed that we also may have something to offer to the larger student affairs profession and to others who work in America's colleges and universities. That is, because we consider Christianity a "view" as well as a "faith," we explore some of the fundamental aspects of the student affairs profession—its history, its relationship to learning, the role of theory—but, we do so within the context of our [Christian] perspective. If, as Bloland, Stamatakos, and Rogers (1995, p. 8) contend, there is really "room in the tent for them [new and innovative paradigms and programs] all," then we hope that our non-Christian counterparts will entertain the notion that a Christian view of higher education in general and the student affairs profession in particular is a plausible alternative.

We mention our struggle with voice in particular because the reader will more than likely notice it. At times, we directly engage our Christian colleagues, perhaps in ways that have no analog among non-Christian professionals. At other points, our intent is to speak more broadly and perspectively, acknowledging that Christians and non-Christians may provide different shape and nuance to underlying principles that we espouse. In either case, and notwithstanding the voice issue, we offer the chapters that follow as a place to begin what we anticipate will be an ongoing discussion as readers pick up the dialog where we left off.

In the first chapter, Terry Thomas and David Guthrie suggest worldviews as a useful means of understanding belief and action. Further, they explore several assumptions about higher education and student affairs based on a Christian point of view, concluding with a brief explanation of the particular Christian worldview that shaped the writing of this book. Realizing that misconceptions about Christian faith proliferate, and likewise that honest differences among Christians exist, we include this chapter in an effort to be clear and honest regarding our point of view as well as its relationship to higher education and student affairs.

The second chapter, written by Barry Loy and William Painter, offers an interpretive history of the student affairs profession in American higher education. More specifically, they include a taxonomy of the historical manifestations of student affairs as well as a critique of each theme within the taxonomy that is informed by a Christian view.

In the third chapter, David Guthrie argues that student affairs must be viewed within the larger context of student learning. The chapter presents several underlying principles of student learning and identifies the ultimate purpose of student learning as wisdom development. Then, in the fourth chapter, he applies these principles and this purpose of student learning to the Christian college context, including how they may shape the work of Christian student affairs professionals.

In the fifth chapter, Jeanette De Jong explores the relationship between a Christian worldview and the role of theory in shaping the efforts of student affairs practitioners. This chapter underscores the importance of theory in the student affairs profession in general, and also challenges Christians in the field with the necessity of critically examining theory through a Christian lens.

The fifth chapter by Jay Barnes and Kate Harrington showcases several model student affairs programs, most of which are consciously shaped by a Christian worldview. Solicited through members of the Association for Christians in Student Development or through other professional contacts, these practices illustrate practical out workings of various ideas presented elsewhere in the book. The final chapter, composed by Kate Harrington, provides summary comments on each of the preceding chapters and charts some possible directions for Christian student affairs professionals to pursue.

Our deepest hopes for this book are twofold. First, that both Christians and those unfamiliar with Christian faith will recognize in these pages that Christian faith involves more than Sunday service; rather, it is a viable wellspring of thoughts and actions, in both public and private spheres, and is clearly within our work as educators. And, second, that those familiar with Christian faith who are also involved in higher education may become more engaged and empowered to undertake their efforts with the understanding that programs offered, classes taught, discipline dispensed, committees formed, counseling offered, friendships nurtured, policies framed, colleagues hired, and so on, are the very arenas in which Christian faith must take shape by God's grace and for God's glory.

David S. Guthrie, Editor
Calvin College
March 1997

References

Bloland, P., Stamatakos, L., & Rogers, R. (1995). Reform in student affairs: A rebuttal to Brown. *ACPA Developments, 22* (5), 8-9.

Bucci, F. (1993). "Student personnel: All hail and farewell!" Revisited. NASPA *Journal, 30* (3), 169-75.

Riggs, L. (1962). *College student personnel work in a Christian context.* Nashville: The Board of Education of the Methodist Church, Division of Higher Education.

Stamatakos, L. & Rogers, R. (1984). Student affairs: A profession in need of a philosophy. *Journal of College Student Personnel, 25* (5), 400-411.

Thomas, D. (1992). Church-related campus culture. In D. Guthrie and R. Noftzger, Jr., (Eds.), *Agendas for church-related colleges and universities* (New Directions for Higher Education, No. 79, pp. 55-63). San Francisco: Jossey-Bass.

Whitt, E., Carnaghi, J., Matkin, J., Scalese-Love, P., & Nestor, D. (1990). Believing is seeing: Alternative perspectives on a statement of professional philosophy for student affairs. *NASPA Journal, 27* (3), 178-84.

Chapter 1

A Framework of Understanding

D. Terry Thomas and David S. Guthrie

THE INDIVIDUALS WHO collaborated to produce this book represent a spectrum of Christian traditions, both personally and institutionally. We were curious regarding how our affiliations as Presbyterians, Baptists, Brethren in Christ, Christian Reformed, and so on would contribute to the effort to consider higher education and student affairs from a Christian point of view. Notwithstanding various and delightful nuances that each of us brought to our discussions, we developed somewhat of what Gilkey (1981, p. 43) referred to as "a shared consciousness, a shared system of meanings."

At the same time, we were concerned about two issues. First, in spite of the spate of authors who suggest that Americans are "at war" culturally, our common experience was that many in contemporary culture are not particularly comfortable or adept at divulging their ultimate allegiances. Whether fearing criticism for "being opinionated" or perhaps simply due to living the proverbial "unexamined life," we sensed that many people were not readily in the business of explaining why they believed what they believed. Second, among our Christian colleagues, we were embarrassingly aware that we infrequently discussed the basic beliefs that give shape to our work and lives. It was not that we felt that we required a steady diet of such conversations, but simply that it may be instructive at times to revisit the nature of our Christian beliefs, particularly as they relate to our vocations.

As a result of our musings, we considered it important to begin the book with this chapter. In it, we present three main topics: (1) a primer on worldview since we believe that worldview is a useful, general framework for understanding beliefs and actions; (2) several preliminary comments regarding the relationship of our [Christian] worldview to higher education and student affairs; and (3) the foundational assumptions of the Christian worldview that

1

has served as the starting point for our own reflections in this book. Though not intended to be exhaustive, we hope that this chapter provides some context for understanding our operational framework as well as the subsequent chapters of the book.

A Primer on Worldview

Student affairs professionals make decisions about issues great and small on a daily basis. Some decisions are personal (What kind of job should I pursue?) and some are professional (What expectations should I have of those whom I supervise?); some decisions are questions of style (How will I model leadership to the students with whom I work?) and some are programmatic (What events can I initiate in the residence halls to promote intended learning outcomes?); and, some decisions are matters of principle (What is the purpose of higher learning, and what contribution will my office make?) while others are simply pragmatic (Who was responsible for the food fight, and what are the consequences?). Quite apart from the specific responses that comprise these decisions, our primary interest is more epistemological, namely: How are these decisions formulated?

Although not new, the concept of worldview maybe a helpful way in which to address this question. A worldview is a comprehensive framework for and interpretive implementation of one's basic beliefs (Walsh and Middleton, 1984; Holmes, 1983). Stated another way, worldviews are "the standard[s] by which reality is managed and pursued" (Olthuis, 1985, p. 155). As such, worldviews are both normative and descriptive (Geertz, 1973). They are normative in the sense that they offer diagnostic understanding of reality and descriptive in the sense that they "bear fruit" as people construct realities.

According to Holmes (1985), worldviews have several characteristics. First, a worldview is "perspectival" in that it orients one's life; it provides perspective to daily reality. Underlying the notion that worldviews are perspectival is an acknowledgment that all people possess ultimate beliefs (Sire, 1994). That is, people naturally "stake their lives on"—they believe in or trust—a particular principle, idea, paradigm, or person. Seen in this light, one might say that all people are "religious," since, as the Latin root (*religio*=restraint) of the word religion suggests, they are "bound" to a particular way of seeing and living life. Believing and doing, in effect, are the essential ingredients of one's worldview.

Second, Holmes (1985, p. 17) characterizes worldviews as "wholistic." Describing a worldview as wholistic refers to both scope and cohesiveness. Regarding scope, a worldview is comprehensive; the entirety of one's existence is in view. Sire's (1988) usage of "universe" to describe the scope of worldview is useful in this regard. With respect to cohesiveness, a worldview serves an integrative function by offering pattern and connection among various dimensions of one's life. For example, how one considers buying and spending, governmental roles, interpersonal relationships, and educational achievement will tend to "hold together." Wolters (1985, p. 3) summarizes this idea succinctly:

> [Worldviews] tend to form a framework or pattern . . . This is not to say that worldviews are never internally inconsistent . . . but it remains true that the more significant feature of worldviews is their tendency toward pattern and coherence; even their inconsistencies tend to fall into clearly recognizable patterns.

Although one's worldview may not be precise in every detail or among details, it provides a foundation upon which one functions in life with a level of confidence, clarity, and consistency. As Gilkey (1981, p. 24) suggests, a worldview "tells us who we are in history and why we are here."

This is not, however, to suggest that worldviews are static. Rather, one's worldview is continually refined and developed. As one's experiences, ideas, ultimate beliefs, and behaviors unfold, his or her worldview takes on new definition and sophistication. At times, a noticeable discontinuity between behavior and belief, an unsettling experience, or exposure to a new idea may even propel a person to explore other worldviews (Walsh, 1992). Whatever the case, a worldview offers a comprehensive, generally cohesive, evolving way to frame one's life.

Finally, Holmes (1985, p. 17) explains that worldviews involve "action outcomes." In contrast to those who may consider a worldview as being solely "what one thinks," we suggest that a worldview includes both the ideas and the actions that reflect one's basic beliefs. Stated another way, worldviews are not only believed but are also "positivized" (Wolters, 1985, p. 15) through opinions, theories, behaviors, actions, and decisions. In a higher education context, this means that how educators define and enact a "good" college, why and how professors evaluate students, why and how residence life programs function, why and how institutions execute assessment programs, why and how colleges maintain athletic programs, and so on, are worldview issues. When educators take time to analyze their efforts, it is often the case that they learn that worldviews are involved, rather than the more simple "culprits" of personalities, traditions, routines, or procedures. Moreover, as Brown (1993, p. 58) suggests, improving higher education will depend in an inordinate way on recognizing that worldviews shape and guide it:

> Changing our higher education system will require a reexamination of its central tenets and most sacred cows. It will require a rethinking of basic ideas, such as: . . . the idea that everyone learns the same way and that the best way of learning disciplined thinking is the academic approach; . . . the idea that tests and papers assess what students know and what they are

becoming; . . . the idea that intellectual competition and the structured search for truth are sufficient dynamics for change within academic institutions to keep them securely ahead of the rest of society.

We discuss worldviews at the outset of this book for two primary reasons. First, we consider worldview a useful means of identifying how people understand, interpret, and construct reality. To reiterate, we believe that the activities of knowing and doing are not undertaken neutrally, but are the products of one's ultimate commitments (Schwehn, 1993). To our mind, worldview is a helpful way of clarifying not only the unavoidable presence of underlying beliefs but the manifestations of them in all areas of life as well.

This leads to a second purpose for introducing the book with worldview, namely, that, as Christians, we cannot suspend our worldview when considering higher education in general or student affairs work in particular. Interpreting our work in colleges has everything to do with our Christian worldview. We admit concomitantly that such an approach may startle some readers who may have heretofore considered Christianity a personal, private issue; a movement compartmentalized to "Christian things" such as theology courses, Sunday worship, chapel programs, regular prayer and Bible study, and seasonal holiday habits; or, a confining—and confounding—litany of dos, don'ts, and damnables. We lament that some are unaware that a Christian view of higher learning and student affairs is even possible. We are equally disappointed that some Christian educators at Christian colleges do not consciously or conscientiously strive to construct and implement learning initiatives that resonate with their ultimate beliefs as Christians. In no small way, this book is intended to enliven a discussion that may address these two concerns.

Worldview, Higher Education, and Student Affairs

Based on the preceding discussion, we argue that a Christian view of higher education in general and student affairs in particular is not only possible but is a natural outworking of basic allegiances; what Christians believe as true is appropriated in what they do. In the same way that structuralist, feminist, critical, or pragmatic views of higher education and student affairs rest on particular assumptions and are interpreted into viable (though perhaps not personally palatable) frameworks and practices, we offer a Christian voice to the larger, contemporary discussion. Moreover, we also want to enliven conversations among our Christian colleagues regarding what and why we think and do in the student affairs profession. Therefore, we offer the following, brief statements as points of departure in framing higher education and student affairs relative to a Christian worldview:

1. Faculty, staff, and students of all institutions of higher learning are cultureformers. Participants of colleges and universities, by their very nature, make sense out of their lives (Sire, 1994), whether in reference to developing a syllabus, choosing a major, developing a residence life program, or initiating a capital campaign.

2. Colleges and universities are neither secular nor sacred. Christian institutions exist as do institutions that do not make such a claim—and legitimately so. People, approaches, events, situations, and decisions that are compatible with a Christian view of life exist at both types of institutions; conversely, people, approaches, and so on that are not compatible with a Christian worldview exist at both types of colleges as well. One would certainly expect that Christian colleges, compared to their nonsectarian counterparts, may evidence considerably more things that are consonant with a Christian point of view.

3. Consciously or unconsciously, intentionally or serendipitously, the business of colleges and universities—Christian and non-Christian—is worldview formation, potential transformation, and nurture (Walsh, 1992). Institutional histories, educational programs, and campus environments offer contextualized experiences that help participants shape, interpret, and enact basic beliefs about and for life. Faculty members, student affairs professionals, and students themselves are integral components of this dynamic process.

4. Colleges, curricula, pedagogies, programs, administrations, learning theories, research laboratories, athletics, and so on are legitimate arenas for faithful [Christian] service. Whether Biblical studies or biology, chapel program or tenure policy, prayer breakfast or curriculum development committee—a Christian worldview suggests the possibility of undertaking these "things" on God's behalf and for God's honor. Similarly, doing student affairs work Christianly has as much to do with the dorm Bible study as it does a disciplinary hearing, as much to do with opening a divisional meeting with prayer as it does with designing an academic support program, and as much to do with a campus-fellowship meeting as it does with a student- government meeting.

5. The learning leadership of Christian colleges must be characterized by discernment, openness, and mutual support. Discernment is necessary to retain distinctiveness; openness is important to avoid separatistic parochialism; and mutual support ensures the type of community in which collaboration, correction, and camaraderie are enhanced.

The Foundations of Our Christian Worldview

Where did these five worldview statements come from? The answer is that they emerged from the basic Christian beliefs that members of our project acknowledge. Before we discuss these assumptions, it is important to admit the elusiveness of the definitive Christian worldview. Full, correct knowledge of God's plan is an impossibility; doing our work as educators completely right is equally unrealistic. Rather, based on the efforts of many others before us, our own Christian traditions and stories, and mutually enriching conversations with one another over several years, we offer what we consider to be the critical components of a Christian worldview that give shape to our lives, our work, and the writing of this book.

Creation

We do not use Creation to signify ecological importance or to emphasize a detailed, cosmological chronology but as a means to underscore several foundational biblical principles on which a Christian understanding of life is based. The first of these principles of the "God-creation relationship" (Holmes, 1985, p. 18) is God's sovereignty. By sovereignty, we simply mean that God is eternal, God authored the created order, and God continues to govern it; sovereignty emphasizes God's presence, power, and rule. A second related principle is that God has intentions for the created order. God desires the created order to develop in ways that conform to God's intentions for it. For example, social relationships are part of God's created order and God has various intentions regarding how they can best occur (e.g., with integrity; love neighbor as one's self). Similarly, God created biological relationships that include an array of provisions about how they best function—fish can breathe underwater and humans cannot (without appropriate scuba gear).

A third principle of the God-creation relationship involves the nature of the created order itself. Positing God's intentions for the created order implies a certain yet-to-be-developed notion. Using the Genesis biblical imagery of a garden, the idea is that God plants a garden with many seeds—personality seeds, family seeds, commerce seeds, social-relationships seeds, education seeds, government seeds, and the like. At the same time, God also envisions the ways in which these seeds may be cultivated most appropriately.

This leads directly to a fourth principle—the role of persons. God created men and women to continue God's initial, creative act by tending the garden. Seen in this light, men and women serve a unique role in the created order as stewards, as ones who "have charge of a master's goods" (Schrotenboer, 1972). In this role, they do more than simply watch the property; they are instructed by God to subdue the created order. The point is further clarified by observing that the word subdue, when translated from the Hebrew *kabash* (Genesis 1:28), means "the development of an effort." Frey, Ingram, McWhertor, and Romanowski (1983, p. 22) summarize the point:

> As a community of "neighbors," our task is to care for and cultivate the reality God formed. The universe is not a self-existent "nature," hostile to

humans, but the realm in which we are to exercise our God-given task of dominion.

The last creational principle may be referred to as the communal dimension of life. God created men and women such that dependence on and care for one another would characterize their personal existence as well as their task to "develop an effort." For example, as applied to education, this principle may suggest that men and women work interdependently to help students discover and continue to discover God's intentions regarding many dimensions of life. Similarly, mutual exchange of ideas and experiences among educators helps to shape their own expanding approximations of what God may have in mind as they cultivate greater wisdom.

Creation is a crucial starting point for coming to terms with our Christian worldview. It provides an important foundation for understanding the relationship between Christianity and society. More specifically, it provides a cue for affirming God's continuing interest in and connection to all areas of life. As applies to our current effort, one may say that we are striving to "develop an effort" in higher education and student affairs that attempts to account for God's desires for them. The biblical concept of Creation, however, is incomplete without also examining the effects of what is typically referred to as the Fall.

Fall

If Creation may be considered the "good news," it is fair to refer to the Fall as the "bad news." As it is used here, the Fall is a reference to Adam's and Eve's disregard of God's sovereignty, as recorded in Genesis 3. Further, according to the scriptural record (Romans 1), all persons who follow as descendants of the "first parents" are predisposed to honor something other than God as the source of authority and direction.

As a result of the Fall, God's created order is significantly and widely distorted. Governments may be abusive and deceitful rather than just; families may be sources of anguish and separation rather than troth; friendships may be based on personal gain or codependence rather than love; schools may be based on competition and reputation rather than on discovery and learning; self-images may be based on performance and pain rather than on God's own image; work may be oppressive and seductive rather than joyful and productive; churches may be places to pose rather than praise; and the list of potential distortions goes on. Because men and women ignore God as the source of and guide for life, life itself is broken rather than whole.

Despite the impact and consequences of the Fall, two observations are noteworthy. First, the Fall does not obliterate God's created order. That is, God continues to exist, God's relationship with creation is not annulled, God's rule of the created order is not usurped, and God's intentions for the created order remain. Using the metaphor from above, God's garden of seeds persists. Further, God's interest in having these seeds be cultivated in appropriate ways (i.e., ways that honor the Creator) remains unabated.

This leads to a second point, namely, that, in spite of the Fall, men and women do not forfeit their roles as stewards. The development of God's created order continues; people retain their identities as cultivators of the created order and continue to develop efforts in every area of life. Because of the Fall, however, men and women may do so in ways that do not reflect God's intentions; because they do not acknowledge God as sovereign, they lack interest in honoring God's desires regarding life. To be clear, it is not that the Fall renders it impossible for men and women to cultivate personalities, relationships, schools, churches, governments, ways of buying and selling, and the like. Rather, men and women now may develop these areas of life without regard for God's intentions. Walsh and Middleton (1984, pp. 70-71) describe the situation as follows:

> As a result [of the Fall], 'the whole creation,' says Paul in Romans 8:19-23, is groaning and waiting for the time when it will be 'liberated from its bondage to decay and brought into the glorious freedom of the children of God.' The creation is waiting, in other words, for *our* liberation . . . Because it [has been] enslaved by our sinful rule, only our redemption will guarantee its freedom.

Is such a restoration, however, even possible? Can men and women recover a relationship with God such that their efforts in developing the created order acknowledge God as the starting point and sustainer of such efforts. Answers to these questions are provided by examining the third critical component of our Christian worldview, namely Redemption.

Redemption

The good news of redemption is that, in spite of the Fall, God does not abandon the God-creation relationship. Rather, the Old and New Testaments of the Bible relate the story of how God progressively reveals a plan of reconciliation and restoration, which climaxes in the life, death, and resurrection of Jesus Christ. According to the scriptural account, Jesus did what Adam and Eve failed to do—he recognized God as sovereign and responded faithfully. Moreover, Jesus' death repairs persons' broken relationships with the Creator, and Jesus' resurrection provides hope and power that their former identities as stewards fulfilling God's intentions may be recovered.

What does this mean in real terms? First, it means that a distorted world is not the last word. Those who trust and follow Jesus do so by striving to approximate God's desires in all areas of their lives—as persons, family members, citizens, worshippers, learners, consumers, and the like. Christians are restored cultivators who attempt to demonstrate what God may have had in mind when envisioning civilization (Wolters, 1985). As relates to this book, being Christian necessitates that we consider higher learning an arena that God not only cares about but about which God also has intentions. As such, we seek to use Christian faith as the lens through which we understand and enact our work in higher education and student affairs.

This leads us to a second consideration. Christians do not possess some special stature, knowledge, or power that makes them privy to the truth in all of its manifestations. As Wells (1989, p. 3) states, "Knowing the 'author of truth' . . . does not insure that we know the truth." Conversely, the Christian view that we have just described also suggests that those who are not Christian may get it right. That is, one need not embrace a Christian worldview to serve God by discovering or implementing something that conforms to God's desires.

The point is simply this: Christians struggle with their non-Christian counterparts with the lingering, ubiquitous effects of the Fall daily in thought, word, and deed; both Christians and non-Christians miss the mark and hit the mark daily in all of the arenas of life. What may distinguish Christians, however, is the freedom that comes from knowing that the Fall is not the final word personally or cosmologically. Moreover, Christians may possess the hope that comes from understanding that God has reenlisted them to be signposts toward shalom in homes, schools, churches, businesses, governments, cities, nations—in all of life (Plantinga, 1990). As relates to Christian student affairs professionals, a Christian view suggests that the profession is a seed within God's garden in which they labor on God's behalf and for God's delight. Their work is further characterized by a sensitivity not only to their own shortcomings viz-à-viz God's desires but to the distortions within the field's theory and practice as well. They work expectantly, however, with an assurance that they are, at any given moment in their thinking about and practice of student affairs, striving to point the way toward what God may have had in mind when God planted the seed called student affairs. Lastly, Christian student affairs practitioners also evaluate what other colleagues—Christian and non-Christian alike—are writing and doing in the field, recognizing that non-Christians may reveal some "good things" and some Christians may uncover some bad things.

A Christian Worldview: A Critique

Although brief, the preceding discussion captures the fundamental components of the beliefs that inform this work. Those familiar with Christian faith in general will surmise that we have high regard for the biblical record, theological and philosophical inquiry, and personal faithfulness. We simultaneously value, however, a qualified, critical stance toward culture, change, ideas, and the like. In short, the Christian worldview that we embrace emphasizes both an allegiance to seek and follow Jesus Christ and a commitment to pursue thoughtfully and diligently what such allegiance means in the context of living in God's world. As such, our Christian worldview does not choose between Jesus and life but affirms the Jesus of life for life.

A Christian worldview as we have described it is most assuredly subject to distortions; after all, the effects of the Fall persist. Past history as well as our own experiences—including those that occurred during the drafting of this book—suggest several potential shortcomings to Christian views, including our own. First, a Christian worldview may be susceptible to triumphalism. That is, if Christians are only diligent enough in their efforts to appropriate God's intentions for politics, education, families, and the like, they will eventually usher in God's perfect kingdom. This distortion overmagnifies the role of persons as redeemed cultivators and minimizes the lingering incompleteness of the created order. We caution that Christians, though from our [Christian] perspective advantaged because of their restored relationship with the Creator, still have imperfect sight. As a result, Christians do well to exercise self-control and humility in their roles as culture-formers on God's behalf.

Second, a Christian worldview may, at times, lack a prophetic stance by failing to offer much conscientious critique of culture writ large or small. Stated another way, Christians may too easily embrace culture without sufficient discernment; if the world belongs to God, why not see it all. We caution against this distortion as well. Balancing, on the one hand, the belief that culture is creationally good and must be cultivated for God's honor, with, on the other hand, the awareness that distortions are manifest throughout culture and must be recognized as such, is not a simple task. Continuous affirmation of God as holy and wise is vital to a Christian worldview in addressing this distortion.

Third, a Christian worldview, as we have explained it here, is potentially susceptible to what may be referred to as pillarism. By pillarism, we mean a tendency to consider one's own traditions to the exclusion of all others. For example, some readers will notice that the Christian worldview that we have outlined is substantially influenced by the Reformed tradition of the Christian faith. Circling the wagons around the Reformed tradition as the right one and concomitantly failing to acknowledge the contributions of other faith traditions is myopic and lacks grace. Although our efforts have been shaped to a significant extent by the Reformed tradition, the diverse denominational composition of the study group challenged us to appreciate the valuable dimensions of other heritages as well. A particular Christian worldview—or any worldview—must never be routine or finished but open to features of other Christian perspectives that provide further understanding, expression, wonder, and truth.

Finally, a Christian worldview, as we have explained it here, may be faulted at times for its tendency to favor scholasticism over community. This is not to say that scholarship emblematic of a Christian worldview is not necessary. On the contrary, we affirm with others that Christian scholarship per se has been scant and weak (Noll, 1994). What is equally disturbing, however, is that compared to the amount of thinking, talking, and writing about Christian views of education, technology, work, psychology, and so on, substantially smaller efforts have gone toward mobilizing, equipping, and sustaining groups of people to live out the principles of a Christian perspective in these same areas of life. For a Christian worldview to have its intended impact, equal efforts must be offered in the support of both scholarship and practice that reflect a Christian point of view.

Conclusion

As we stated at the outset, in framing this book, we believed that it would be incomplete—and perhaps confusing—without briefly acknowledging and outlining a worldview framework in general and our own Christian starting point in particular. We reiterate that how we construct meaning about higher learning and student affairs in the chapters that follow is shaped by the Christian worldview that we have briefly offered here. To be sure, this chapter may raise a myriad of questions, comments, and arguments among non-Christians and Christians alike. To the extent that it does, we consider that we are off to a good start.

References

Brown, E. (1993). *An American imperative: Higher expectations for higher education, A Contributed Essay.* Racine, WI: The Wingspread Group on Higher Education, The Johnson Foundation, Inc.

Frey, B., Ingram, W., McWhertor, T., & Romanowski, W. (1983). *All of life redeemed: Biblical insight for daily obedience.* Jordan Station, Ontario: Paideia Press.

Geertz, C. (1973). *The interpretation of cultures.* New York: Basic Books.

Gilkey, L. (1981). *Society and the sacred: Toward a theology of culture in decline.* New York: Crossroad.

Holmes, A. (1983). *Contours of a worldview.* Grand Rapids: Eerdmans.

Holmes, A. (1985). Toward a Christian view of things. In A. Holmes (Ed.), *The making of a Christian mind: A Christian worldview and the academic enterprise* (pp. 11-28). Downers Grove: InterVarsity Press.

Noll, M. (1994). *The scandal of the evangelical mind.* Grand Rapids: Eerdmans.

Olthuis, J. (1985). On worldviews. *Christian Scholars Review, 14* (2), 153-64.

Plantinga, C. (1990 March 6). *Educating for shalom.* Paper presented at a meditation for freshman honors students, Calvin College, Grand Rapids, MI.

Schrotenboer, P. (1972). *Man in God's world.* Toronto: Wedge Publishing Foundation.

Schwehn, M. (1993). *Exiles in Eden: Religion and the academic vocation in America.* New York: Oxford University Press.

Sire, T. (1994). *Why should anyone believe anything at all.* Downers Grove: InterVarsity Press.

Sire, T. (1988). *The universe next door* (2d ed.). Downers Grove: InterVarsity Press.

Walsh, B. (1992). Worldviews, modernity, and the task of Christian college education, *Faculty Dialogue, 18*, 13-35.

Walsh, B., & Middleton, R. (1984). *The transforming vision: Shaping a Christian worldview*. Downers Grove: InterVarsity Press.

Wells, R. (1989). *History through the eyes of faith: Western civilization and the kingdom of God*. San Francisco: Harper & Row.

Wolters, A. (1985). *Creation regained: Biblical basics for a reformational worldview*. Grand Rapids: Eerdmans.

Chapter 2

Student Affairs in Historical Perspective

Barry J. Loy and William M. Painter

THIS CHAPTER IS concerned with the historical development of the student affairs profession. More specifically, we identify five particular periods of this development as follows: (1) student affairs as spiritual development (1636-1860); (2) student affairs as humanitarian guidance (1860-1925); (3) student affairs as student personnel and services (1925-1960); (4) student affairs as developmental science (1960-1985); and (5) student affairs in transition (1985-present). Although overlap undoubtedly exists, we believe that this approach provides a helpful tool in understanding how the profession has taken shape since higher education was incorporated in this country in 1636. Following a discussion of selected issues within each time period, we offer a brief, reflective analysis.

Ours is clearly not the first, most comprehensive, or best history of the student affairs profession. We include this chapter, however, because we believe that other such histories have been less than interpretive and much less critical of historical developments within the profession. In contrast, we began with Wells' (1989, p. 8) reminder that: "The facts of history simply do not speak for themselves; historians speak for them from an interpretive framework of the ideas they already hold." As a result, we started this chapter expecting to interpret some of the profession's historical development as appropriate and some of it as wrongheaded. Moreover, given the intent of the book, we strove to frame such interpretations based on a Christian view of life. Although to some readers—and even to ourselves at times—our critical interpretation may not seem uniquely Christian, we did struggle to use a Christian lens to make sense of the complex issues that accompany the emergence and maturation of the student affairs profession. From our perspective, the combination of critical interpretation and a Christian view makes this history of the profession a distinctive one.

Student Affairs as Spiritual Development (1636-1860)

Overview

Although the student affairs profession as we know it in the late twentieth century did not exist in America's colonial colleges, educators during this period were committed to what is commonly referred to today as the development of the "whole student." In-class and out-of-class learning were intended to develop pious and disciplined young men who would serve the colonies as ecclesiastical and civic leaders. Ryken (1987, p. 43) summarizes:

> [The goal of the early colleges] was the education of the whole person, morally and spiritually as well as intellectually. Both the curriculum and the campus climate were governed by a religious purpose aimed at the glory of God and the Christian nurture of the student, by a tone of moral earnestness, and by an antisecular bias that refused to separate education from religious concerns.

During this period of higher education, educating the mind was not distinct from nurturing the spirit. Intellectual growth was not properly achieved without a concomitant cultivation of the spiritual life. The incorporating Statutes of Harvard make it clear that students were expected to "by prayer in secret, seek wisdom of Him" and to "exercise himself in reading Scriptures twice a day . . . seeing the Entrance of the word giveth light" (Goodchild & Wechsler, 1989, p. 89). The inseparable linkage between mind and spirit was not only educationally orthodox but was the sine qua non to the development of a new civilization that would provide light to the world (Marsden, 1994).

Early instructors used the entire campus environment—classroom and residence—to realize their educational aims. In the classroom, the trivium (grammar, rhetoric, and dialectic) and quadrivium (arithmetic, geometry, astronomy, and arts) provided ample "furniture of the mind" while fastidious language studies, biblical studies, and class recitations "disciplined the mind" (Goodchild & Wechsler, 1989).

Out of the classroom, educators continued their supervision of students' learning. Operating as surrogate parents, which was simplified because tutors and students often lived in common quarters, they enforced strict discipline and required the performance of religious duties. Each school day began and ended with prayer; worship was mandatory. Rules governing hunting, sailing, spending money, sleeping, and showing respect were maintained dutifully, often resulting to strained relationships between students and faculty (Harrington, 1992). Punishments for violating these codes included fines, loss of privileges, public confessions, flogging, and expulsions (Ringenberg, 1984; Rudolph, 1962).

Despite the emergence of several nascent extracurricular activities in the late eighteenth century, including literary societies and the first Phi Beta Kappa fraternity at William and Mary in 1776 (Ringenberg, 1984), the classical education model originally embodied by the colonial colleges persisted for over two hundred years. Although several notable institutional innovations developed by the mid-nineteenth century, the Yale Report of 1828 and the proliferation of denominational colleges with westward expansion (Tewksbury, 1932) helped to sustain the hegemonic influence of the "piety and discipline" (Veysey, 1964) model of student learning.

Commentary

During this period, higher education reflected the relative ideological homogeneity of early American culture, offering what may be considered a unified or wholistic experience (Rothblatt, 1993). As a matter of course, faith and learning were related, knowing and doing were connected, and in-class and out-of-class learning were equally necessary. To romanticize this period of American higher education, however, fails to account for some of the disturbing aspects of these early colleges. For example, they were largely elitist institutions, excluding women, people of color, and those who may not have fit the religious, cultural, or financial picture of those managing the development of the "new world." One wonders what may have transpired if, during this period, college leadership had considered the preservation of tradition and the transformation of society differently.

Although the academy during this period was decidedly religious, and Christianly so, it also operated, to a large degree, with an uncritical acceptance of the medieval synthesis of Greek and biblical worldviews. That is, Christian educators believed that Christian education involved exhorting students to know and learn rightly the right things through the right means, such that right leadership would result and a *godly* society would eventually emerge. This synthesis of Christian faith and reason was the context from which later conflicts in the academy emerged. For example, by the end of the eighteenth century, Noll (1994) suggests that a new moral philosophy developed in which reason began to supplant revelation as the appropriate path to the *good* society; the reason component of the faith-reason synthesis became increasingly prominent. As numerous authors have chronicled (Noll, 1994; Marsden, 1994; Schwehn, 1993), the virtual disestablishment of Christian faith in the academy would ultimately eventuate.

Student Affairs as Humanitarian Guidance (1860-1925)

Overview

Between the mid-nineteenth century and the early twentieth century, major developments occurred in American higher education. Although traditional liberal arts colleges continued to be founded during this period, two other types of institutions gained prominence: the land grant university and the research university. The Morrill Land Grant Act of 1862 provided for the sale of federal lands to help establish state universities. In turn, these land-grant universities pledged to offer curricular programs in agriculture and the mechanical arts as a means of responding to the nascent technological needs of an expanding and developing society. Given its intent "to promote the liberal and practical education of the industrial classes in the several pursuits and professions in life" (Hofstadter & Smith, 1961, p. 568), the institutions founded under the Morrill Act developed new curricula, attracted more diversified student populations, and required more specific professorial preparation.

Chronologically on the heels of the land grant movement was "the emergence of the American university" (Veysey, 1964). Borrowing from the German university model which emphasized knowledge discovery through unfettered scientific research, educational leaders pioneered what Charles Eliot (1869), forty year president of Harvard, referred to as a "new education." Johns Hopkins University, founded in 1876, is typically regarded as the first institution founded on the new education, which its first president characterized as follows:

> that the institution now taking shape should forever be free from the influences of ecclesiasticism or partisanship, as those terms are used in narrow and controversial senses; that all departments of learning,—mathematical, scientific, literary, historical, philosophical,—should be promoted, as far as the funds at command will permit, the new departments of research receiving full attention, while the traditional are not slighted; that the instructions should be as thorough, as advanced and as special as the intellectual condition of the country will permit; that the glory of the University should rest upon the character of the teachers and scholars here brought together . . . . It is their researches in the library and the laboratory; their utterances in the classroom and in private; their example as students and investigators, and as champions of the truth; their publications, through the journals and the scientific treatises, which will make the University of Baltimore an attraction to the best students, and serviceable to the intellectual growth of the land (Hofstadter & Smith, 1961, pp. 755-56).

The development of American research universities also precipitated significant institutional changes. During this period, new disciplines and subdisciplines emerged, new academic departments ossified around these curricular changes, faculty members pursued increasingly greater specialization, professional scholarly associations were born, and student enrollments burgeoned (Geiger, 1986). At the same time, Schwehn (1993) suggests that many educators became considerably less interested in addressing questions about the meaning of "the whole" or the overarching purposes of human life. Similarly, many faculty members were becoming distracted by registration, advising, and counseling functions (Garland, 1985) as well as students' growing interest in the increased availability of extracurricular activities such as intercollegiate athletics, fraternities, literary societies, and student publications (Rudolph, 1962).

Given this context, perhaps it comes as little surprise that the student affairs profession emerged during this period. President Eliot of Harvard appointed the first student dean in 1870. Although he performed other administrative functions related to instruction, student records, and registration, the primary responsibility of the first dean, Ephraim Gurney, was to take the burden of student discipline from President Eliot (Garland, 1985). Clearly, this function of the profession has persisted into the modern era.

During the early years of the twentieth century, the fledgling profession mirrored the professionalization of academe writ large. The titles of Dean of Men and Dean of Women appeared at this time, most frequently at the larger institutions. The University of Chicago is generally regarded as the first institution to use the title, Dean of Women, in 1892 (Horowitz, 1987), although the first holder of the title, Alice Freeman Palmer, conferred the title and the duties of the post to her associate, Marion Talbot, due to Palmer's frequent travels (Fley, 1979). Thomas Arkle Clark was the first to claim the title, Dean of Men, which occurred at The University of Illinois in 1909. According to Fley (1979), Clark became widely known as an expert on student life and the problems of high-school and college men.

In these early days of the profession, student deans helped make college life for students compatible with institutional goals and worked with student leaders to coordinate various extracurricular activities (Horowitz, 1987). Moreover, because of their own religious predispositions, many of these professionals were considerably interested in students' character development. For example, Thomas Arkle Clark, mentioned above, was an elder in the Presbyterian church and assumed that efforts to encourage character development were a natural part of the purpose of higher learning (Fley, 1979). Similarly, Stanley Coulter, who became the dean of men at Purdue University in 1919 following a long and successful tenure as the dean of the School of Science, exhorted the audience of the National Association of Deans and Advisers of Men not to take their work lightly because "you are not dealing with mechanisms, you are dealing with these beings Almighty God created to finish His unfinished work on earth" (Fley, 1980, p. 25). Rhatigan (1978, p. 13) summarized the identities of a majority of these early professionals:

[They were] persons having high ideals, warmth, optimism, and genuineness. They appear to have enjoyed the respect of and to have shown ᵢaffection, compassion, and concern for students. Most of them were deeply religious; it is interesting to observe that most came from backgrounds in the liberal arts; our kinship with the liberal arts is a facet of our history that warrants more careful examination and articulation.

A commitment to students' character development rooted within a Christian worldview, however, was not the universal approach for all of the early student affairs professionals. According to Young, many entered the new field simply because "they wanted to help other people" (1993a, p. 244).

By the third decade of the twentieth century and given the evolution of academe as a whole, student affairs professionals felt pressure both to professionalize and to identify a scientific basis for their work. Although the professionalization of the field as well as its scientific rootedness did not fully occur until later, the beginnings of each surfaced during this period and, at the expense of jumping ahead, warrant several brief comments.

With respect to the professionalization of the field, the National Association of Deans of Women (NADW) began in 1916 (Fley, 1979), soon followed by the founding of the National Association of Deans of Men (NADM) in 1917 (Cowley, 1964). By the next year, members of the NADM decided to "hold a little conference" (Turner, 1968, p. 33) to discuss informally various issues relevant to their work, including "social activities, fraternities, scholarship, housing, health, and student government" (Young, 1993a, p. 245). Although it was not until 1930 that the National Association of Student Personnel Administrators (NASPA) officially received its name and charter, the inchoate "little conferences" reflected the movement toward increasing professionalization. Similarly, the founding of the National Association of Placement and Personnel Officers in 1924, which became the American College and Personnel Association (ACPA) seven years later, evidenced a growing interest to gather student affairs deans, counselors, and extrainstructional practitioners for the purpose of further defining, shaping, and improving their work (Cowley, 1964).

The inauguration of the first master of arts degree for deans of women in 1914 at Columbia University Teachers College contributed to the sophistication of the fledgling profession. This program was based on Dewey's instrumentalist philosophy, both reflecting and, eventually, a reflection of the predisposition and practices of early student affairs practitioners to serve people and solve problems (Schetlin, 1968; Lloyd-Jones & Smith, 1954). Courses in the program included "child and adolescent hygiene, sex education, educational psychology, family history, educational sociology, educational philosophy, school management, administrative problems, the psychology of religion, and a practicum" (Young 1993a, p. 245). It is interesting to note that men were not admitted to this program until 1928, at which time the name of the program became student personnel administration (Lloyd-Jones, 1949).

With regard to establishing a scientific foundation for its work, the profession turned to the fields of counseling and testing during this period. Whereas the testing emphasis was adopted from its most prevalent use within the military, the counseling focus sprang from the guidance movement within secondary education. Since guidance, however, had potentially limiting connotations given its authoritarian and religious nuances, the profession readily moved toward counseling as a more acceptable motif for the profession during this period and beyond (Cowley, 1964).

Commentary

The emergence of a young student affairs profession during this period, on one hand, was a positive development in several regards. At a time in which many faculty members were beginning to be more exclusively interested in their immediate classroom context and the advancement of knowledge (Geiger, 1986), these early student affairs practitioners helped to maintain more personal, informal contact with students. Many of them embraced an interest in students' spiritual development. Many of them wished to maintain a synergistic balance between students' intellectual development (since most of them were full professors) and students' character development. Many of them were concerned to do their work better, precipitating commitments to collaboration and improved scientific understanding of students. Many of them wished to perpetuate the apparent wholism of the early era despite the growing fragmentation of disciplines, departments, and functions within the academe.

The advent of the student affairs profession, on the other hand, though begun in part to offset the atomization occurring within institutions of higher learning, created its own sort of reductionism. That is, though committed to maintaining a cohesive educational experience for students, the early student affairs profession, in retrospect, may have contributed to greater fragmentation. In this regard, we offer two observations. First, although most student affairs staff during this period were distinguished faculty members, over time, student affairs professionals became just that—professionals. The professionalization of the functions of student affairs eventually led to the marginalization—and, in some ways, the self-marginalization—of the profession from the overall educational enterprise. As professions typically evolve, then, student affairs developed its own language, differentiated titles, professional associations, specialized subfunctions, theory base, career orbits, and the like—at times with a seeming disregard for the larger context of student learning within which it existed.

Second, as a function of the movement toward professionalization, the responsibility for guidance or counseling captured many student affairs staff during this period. Many of these early deans were motivated by Christian convictions and thus, in their work, attempted to encourage the development of character and morality in students. At the same time, they were not immune from the trend within higher education toward a naturalistic world, a knowable universe with design but without the need for revelation or a Designer. The "secularization of the academy" (Marsden & Longfield, 1992) created dissonance for Christian student affairs professions who were committed to personal beliefs and student morality, on the one hand, and to an emerging profession and credibility with the institution, on the other. In retrospect, this tension produced various results. Some professionals eschewed Christian moorings while retaining a nonbiblically rooted interest in students' character development; some professionals preserved Christian principles and interpreted student affairs work as ministry; some professionals, Christian and non-Christian alike, apotheosized professional credibility as the cardinal—and neutral—value; and, so it goes. One wonders how the tensions among Christian faith, the purpose of student affairs work, educational cohesion, and professional credibility might be navigated. From our perspective, the question continues today.

Student Affairs as Student Personnel and Services (1925-1960)

Overview

If student affairs in the previous period might be described as humanitarians beginning a profession, the next period finds student affairs firmly establishing itself as a profession of personnel specialists. Not only were the two primary professional organizations for student affairs practitioners of today—ACPA and NASPA—founded during this period, many graduate programs emerged as well, providing training particularly in psychological testing and counseling techniques (Schetlin, 1968). Perhaps the most significant contribution toward the professionalization of student affairs at this time, however, was the development and codification of professional "points of view" (NASPA, 1989).

The ACPA Committee on Personnel Principles and Functions, in 1931, delineated the nature of student affairs work (Saddlemire & Rentz, 1986). In their ground breaking work, the committee gave definition to the profession as follows:

> Personnel work in a college or university is the systematic bringing to bear on the individual student all those influences, of whatever nature, which will stimulate him and assist him, through his own efforts, to develop in body, mind and character to the limit of his individual capacity for growth, and helping him to apply his powers so developed most effectively to the work of the world (Clothier, 1931, p. 10).

Six years later, the Executive Committee of the American Council on Education appointed a group of educators to report on the state of "personnel work" in higher education. The comprehensive report issued by the committee became known as the Student Personnel Point of View (NASPA, 1989). The document reminded its readers that, until the latter part of the nineteenth century, interest in the whole student had dominated the thinking of the educational leaders of America's colleges and universities. Criticizing the fragmentation that had occurred in higher education since that time, the report affirmed wholistic education and encouraged institutions to give equal emphasis to the development of the person and the development of the mind. The Student Personnel Point of View (NASPA, 1989, p. 49):

> imposes upon educational institutions the obligation to consider the student as a whole—his intellectual capacity and achievement, his emotional make up, his physical condition, his social relationships, his vocational aptitudes and skills, his moral and religious values, his economic resources, and his aesthetic appreciations. It puts emphasis, in brief, upon the development of the student as a person rather than upon his intellectual training alone.

The "personnel perspective" provided a useful framework for the maturing profession to address the needs of the large influx of students following World II, many of whom were military veterans. It provided useful direction to deans and counselors interested in "giving [college] boys a philosophy which will enable them to meet the present situation" (NADAM, 1943, p. 28). Moreover, given the widening gap between academic affairs and student affairs precipitated in part by substantial expansion, disciplinary specialization, and the hegemony of the research economy (Geiger, 1986), the Student Personnel Point of View of 1937 offered a means of authenticating the profession within higher education.

The profession's place to stand was strengthened further by a subsequent statement from the American Council on Education in 1949. This 1949 version of the Student Personnel Point of View reaffirmed the development of the whole person as the central value of the profession but advocated broader educational goals for democracy, international understanding, and solving social problems. Given the clientele entering college as well as the national sentiment borne by the recently completed global conflict, it comes as little surprise that the revised statement included such nuances. Both statements, however, are very clear regarding the belief that "learning is centered in the institution, not just in the classroom" (Allen & Garb, 1993, pp. 94-95).

By the mid-1950s, many student affairs professionals were managing services that addressed students' personal and academic adjustment needs, including opportunities to participate in extracurricular opportunities. Despite the student-centered and service-oriented disposition of many student affairs staff, some of them lacked adequate training in the areas in which they served, particularly since World War II had depleted the numbers of student personnel graduate students in deference to military service. Notwithstanding these possible training deficiencies, the profession continued to cohere and would sooñ experience substantial intellectual invigoration from the theories and practices that emerged during the next three decades.

Before offering several critical remarks about this time period, it is fitting to comment briefly about the organizing that was occurring among the student affairs practitioners of church-related and independent Christian colleges. Compared to their nonsectarian counterparts, these institutions retained mission statements and institutional practices evidencing a commitment to Christian education. For example, the vast majority of these colleges maintained biblical/theological studies as part of the general education requirement, required faculty members to acknowledge a Christian faith commitment, and continued compulsory chapel attendance (Ringenberg, 1984). Similar to the colonial colleges, the church-related colleges and independent Christian colleges of the 1950s considered intellectual development and spiritual development equally important.

The student affairs staff of these institutions desired ideas and advice regarding their professional service that concomitantly accounted for their commitment to the Christian faith. To that end, the student affairs deans of several of these colleges met in Chicago in 1957 to discuss the possibility of a professional association for Christian student affairs practitioners. Their planning resulted in the launching of the Christian Association of Deans of Women (CADW) and the Association of Christian Deans and Advisors of Men (ACDAM) in 1958. Both organizations held their first meetings at Fort Wayne Bible College (Fort Wayne, Indiana) to develop and ratify their respective constitutions. According to Zopfi (1991, p. 6), "these organizations grew out of a desire to hear speakers and to receive information that would be helpful to them in the Christian schools in which they were working." Although some of these Christian professionals attended the annual association meetings of NASPA and ACPA, they also desired connection with colleagues with whom they shared similar personal beliefs and institutional context.

Commentary

Two curious ironies are evident in this period of development for the student affairs profession. First, despite the clear commitment to learning and whole-person development expressed in the profession's two primary statements (1937, 1949), the profession's niche within the expanding and atomizing higher education arena became more and more defined as that of support-service providers. Although this may be understandable given the large influx of students after World War II as well as the sizeable amounts of federal funding provided to institutions to service these students, one wonders whether student affairs professionals, in the race to be valued within the academy, too quickly accepted these service roles. What may have been lost in the process was the opportunity to establish themselves—in their own eyes as well as in the eyes of their classroom faculty colleagues—as coparticipants in the educational enterprise. Allen and Garb (1993, pp. 94, 97) summarize the point:

> [The profession's) traditions grew out of being student-centered and service-oriented. Our initial attachment to the institutional organizational structure was through services not necessarily focused on learning . . . . As we have tried to diminish our marginality, we have abdicated our role as active shapers of learning-centered education, that includes character formation as well as the transmission of information.

The second irony, related to the first, is that the professionalization of student affairs may have had the reverse effect of what was originally intended. The establishment of associations and graduate programs and the creation of a student personnel point of view ostensibly may have prepared student affairs professionals not only to be copartners in student learning but to be active participants in encouraging the academy to embrace a more wholistic approach to education. What occurred, however, was that the specialization that the student affairs profession ultimately pursued paralleled the specialization that the profession had initially critiqued in the academy writ large. Although the profession professed commitment to wholistic learning, its own professionalization combined with the concomitant professionalization of academic departments resulted in a bifurcated approach to higher education in Christian and non-Christian institutions alike: faculty members were teachers and student affairs staff were "control agents and social directors" (Allen & Garb, 1993, p. 95).

Student Affairs as Developmental Science (1960-1985)
Overview

The student affairs profession expanded its functions as the numbers of students enlarged and diversified during the 1960s. The Civil Rights and women's movements improved access to higher education for ethnic minority and women students. Baby boomers reached college age as well, and enrollments across the country doubled by the early 1970s. In addition, although the Vietnam War raged, "there was no dearth of students in higher education" (Young, 1993a, p. 247) as there had been during the two World Wars. To meet these burgeoning student numbers, student affairs departments grew in the areas of admissions, housing, food service, student activities, counseling, orientation, minority advising, and support services for the physically and learning disabled (Garland, 1985).

At the same time, graduate programs in student personnel reached their peak period around 1970 (Task Force, 1991), having also expanded the canon of effective professional preparation beyond familiarity with testing and counseling techniques (Etheridge, 1967; Lloyd-Jones, 1968). New residence halls required new residence hall staff to supervise and lead the larger student populations—despite the eclipse of in loco parentis—and graduate schools helped to provide them. In addition, beginning in the 1960s, the profession improved its heretofore theoretical base by borrowing liberally from the fields of psychology and sociology. In a later chapter, we will discuss this issue in greater detail. For now, we simply wish to note that two professional associations issued substantive, theory-driven statements during this period. Reflecting Chickering's (1969) seminal work in the field, both documents exhorted the student affairs profession to make human development the center of its ideology and practice.

The first statement, produced by the American College Personnel Association (ACPA) in 1975, was called the Tomorrow's Higher Education project (THE). It championed "student development" as the appropriate guiding philosophy for the profession. The THE project defined student development as the application of human-development concepts (patterned, orderly lifelong processes leading to self-determination and self-direction) in the postsecondary context (ACPA, 1975). According to the document, embracing student development as the field's raison d'etre would require a reconceptualization of the profession, theory-based goal setting, proactive interventions, and rigorous evaluation.

The Council of Student Personnel Associations in Higher Education (COSPA) issued a second important statement, also in 1975. Similar to ACPA's treatise, COSPA's Student Development Services in Post Secondary Education (COSPA, 1975) emphasized students' unlimited potential for development and self-direction. Becoming expert in human development theory was the sine qua non to effective professional planning and practice. According to the COSPA statement, the appropriate function of a student affairs practitioner was as a student-development specialist, or, as Zaccaria (1968, p. 104) had stated almost a decade earlier, an "applied behavioral scientist." In contrast to their faculty colleagues who emphasized content, the natural interest of student affairs professionals was process.

The conclusions expressed in these statements were not entirely new. The general concept of whole-person development dated back at least to the student-personnel-point-of-view documents, if not to the colonial colleges. The student development movement, however, was unique for at least two reasons. First, it insisted on the utilization of student development theories to inform practice. Bloland, Stamatakos, and Rogers (1994, p. 3) make this clear:

> what was purportedly new about the student development movement was that first, university staff should intentionally introduce "proactive" programs, called interventions, to promote student development; and, second, that the nature and content of these interventions and their outcomes could be specified by designing them in conformance with an appropriate theory of human development.

The second distinctive feature of the student development movement was simply its unprecedented allure; student development had a certain "sex appeal" that previous ideals lacked. Student affairs graduate programs picked up the phrase with considerable enthusiasm in the 1970s and early 1980s. Student development became the umbrella for research on an array of student-related topics as well as for programmatic initiatives. At a time in which the profession was eager to achieve greater respect in a specialized, academic environment, the theme of student development could not have come at a more opportune time. Christian student affairs professionals were influenced sufficiently by the movement to dissolve the Christian Association of Deans of Women (CADW) and the Association of Christian Deans and Advisors of Men (ACDAM) in favor of one organization that became known as the Association for Christians in Student Development (ACSD) in 1980. Virtually without critique but with much fanfare, the student development movement enjoyed widespread acceptance among student affairs professionals in both Christian and non-Christian institutional contexts.

Commentary

That little debate occurred about the acceptance of the student development as the operational framework for the student affairs profession is not to suggest that it was unassailable. We suggest several weaknesses. First, as we have suggested elsewhere, the profession's desire for recognition and status within the academy was a driving force behind its historical development. Such longing for credibility, which typically took the form of mimicking faculty's interests in specialization, professionalization, and scientific respectability, mitigated against the alleged interest of the student affairs profession to encourage integrality in the learning experience. Mouthing wholistic student development, on the one hand, and practicing fragmentation with respect to tasks, programs, and theories on the other, did little to advance the cause of a cohesive student learning.

A second and related critique is that, although it appeared to be a cohesive metatheory within the profession, the student development movement was more accurately a loose collection of many hypotheses regarding young adult development. That is, irrespective of the particular characteristic of a student's development that a view highlighted, it became subsumed under the heading of student development. In effect, the student development movement was a "the whole equals the sum of its parts" approach, or, as Bloland, Stamatakos, and Rogers (1994) suggest, a "more seam than coat" approach. Rather than provide an overarching, wholistic framework for understanding and interpreting student learning, student development was a convenient catchall for the disparate assortment of psychosocial and ecological theories having something to do with human development. Instead of accomplishing the intended theoretical and practical cohesiveness in the profession, much less the academy as a whole, the student development movement may actually have contributed to a more fragmented understanding of student learning.

Third, student development discussions frequently occurred outside of the context of student learning. With the ascendancy of the student development movement, the student affairs profession ostensibly created its own conversation about college students as if the students were not in college. That is, dialog about students' cognitive, moral, emotional, faith, and sexual development occurred as if the locale for such development was irrelevant. The recent release of the Student Learning Imperative (1994) continues to reflect such a view. Although the writers suggest that development and learning are synonymous, they continue to use both terms together (i.e., student learning and development) throughout the document. Either the architects of the treatise are prone to redundancy or, more likely, they embrace a dual context for the college experience—one that is called student development that predominantly occurs outside the classroom and is supervised by student affairs professionals, and one that is called student learning that mostly takes place inside the classroom and is overseen by faculty members.

Finally, we suggest that, similar to their non-Christian colleagues, Christians in the student affairs profession also adopted the student development movement. Enamored by its student-centeredness, its emphasis on personal development, and its potential to provide a sufficient elixir with respect to gaining greater respect institutionally (since a chasm also existed between student affairs and academic affairs in Christian colleges), Christian professionals accepted student development philosophy as the Christian approach. Although we readily concede that students develop intellectually, socially, and so on both inside and outside of the classroom during their college years, we argue that a Christian view suggests the integrality of the college learning experience rather than the sum-of-the-parts approach typified by the student development movement. Moreover, even if a sum-of-the-parts approach was acceptable, Christian professionals must distinguish themselves, in part, by discerning the components of a particular theory, practice, or approach that resonate with their beliefs and those that do not.

Student Affairs in Transition (1985-present)

Overview

Since the mid-1980s, American higher education has experienced considerable change, often the result of public scrutiny and subsequent critique. Increasing costs, shrinking federal aid, and greater competition for students have necessitated that colleges and universities right size, rethink financial aid, and develop attractive marketing agendas. In addition, legal liabilities, accreditation pressures, and new economies have helped to capture institutions' attention regarding the importance of conflict management, assessment, and strategic planning. That self-proclaimed optimist and longtime student of higher education Clark Kerr (1994) is less than sanguine as he writes *Troubled Times Ahead for American Higher Education* is, at the very least, worth noting. Although he does not predict a third great transformation in higher education (Kerr, 1991), Kerr does forecast continuing change that will require educational leaders to be adaptable, savvy, and cooperative.

The student affairs profession clearly was not immune from these developments. Student affairs divisions participated with other institutional leaders in evaluating existing programs, developed new initiatives to enhance institutional image and improve student success, and discussed strategies for the best allocation of available resources. Practitioners worked harder at interdivisional collaboration with faculty colleagues, shifted efforts to programs that would bolster student retention, and probed means of eliminating the duplication of effort regarding both support staff and professional staff functions. In some cases, student affairs divisions were dissolved as such in an effort to reconfigure and improve the delivery of the most important student services (Davenport, Roscoe, & Brandell, 1995). In short, the student affairs profession adopted a political stance (Allen & Garb, 1993) in an effort to preserve and maximize their standing in a fluctuating educational environment. NASPA's reexamination of the student personnel point of view characterized this stance. The statement that resulted in 1987, entitled "A Perspective on Student Affairs," reflected the profession's moving away from the student development approach toward a strategic positioning of itself within the academy. An excerpt from the document illustrates the point (NASPA, 1989, p. 13):

> Colleges and universities organize their primary activities around the academic experience: the curriculum, the library, the classroom, and the laboratory. The work of student affairs should not compete with and cannot substitute for that academic experience. As a partner in the educational enterprise, student affairs enhances and supports the academic missions.

The authors seemed to be aware that attempting to elevate the role of student affairs by emphasizing its own student development philosophy and practice was ultimately neither successful nor helpful. Rather than operate its own agenda of student development in reaction to the academic program, perhaps the profession was wise to identify itself as being in harmony with the faculty in realizing the broader educational mission of the institution. Given the higher education environment since the mid-1980s in which competition for resources and an emphasis on quality were vital, supporting the academic mission rather than substituting for it was politically astute.

At the same time, a slew of books championed the role of student affairs practitioners as partners with faculty colleagues in the educational experience. Astin's (1985) "talent development" model and "involvement theory" presupposed collaboration with the academic division. Similarly, *New Futures for Student Affairs* (Barr, Upcraft, & Associates, 1990), *Involving Colleges* (Kuh, Schuh, Whitt, & Associates, 1991), *How College Affects Students* (Pascarella & Terenzini, 1992), *What Matters in College* (Austin, 1993), and *Education and Identity* (Chickering & Reisser, 1993)—all required reading for today's professionals—identified the integrality of the student affairs profession in relationship to the overall learning enterprise. In short, over the last ten years, the profession has positioned itself—at least theoretically—more strategically than during the previous period as an important contributor to the realization of an institution's mission.

Bloland, Stamatakos, and Rogers (1994) have made a case more recently for strengthening the profession's connection with institutions' academic missions. Their recommendations, however, are more specific—and ambitious—than those offered in the 1987 NASPA document. They suggest that the student affairs profession do the following:

1. Cease identifying with the student development model as the well-spring . . . of the field of student affairs.

2. Return to the general principles . . . expressed in the Student Personnel Point of View . . . clearly placing academic and intellectual development at the center of the student affairs mission.

3. Re-emphasize the primacy of learning as the cardinal value of higher education

4. Clearly identify with the institutional educational mission . . .

5. Seek ways to participate more fully in the academic life of the parent college or university, distinctly identifying the contribution that student affairs can and does make to implementing institutional educational purposes (1994, pp. 104-5).

If Bloland, Stamatakos and Rogers encourage student affairs practitioners to emphasize students' intellectual development, others call for the profession to highlight students' character development. For example, reacting against the values neutrality of the 1960s and 1970s, Young (1993b) identifies a resurgence of interest in values-driven interventions and programs. Such a rekindled interest may recapture the approach of many earlier professionals who naturally assumed that their role included providing some moral guidance to students during the college years. Young is not hesitant to include one chapter (Dalton, 1993), however, that warns against an association between character development and the transmission of religious values. Although eschewing mindless indoctrination as well, we suggest that helping to shape a student's character is not only a legitimate role of a college educator (including a student affairs professional) but is to be undertaken in a morally directive rather than a morally neutral manner (Schwehn, 1993).

Commentary

During the last ten years, the student affairs profession's expressions of commitment to the educational mission are laudable. Even if seen in the worst possible light, namely as a means of protecting itself in times of more scarce resources and more fastidious program review, it reflects an awareness of the current political environment in which many colleges and universities find themselves. Having greater awareness of the larger institutional context in which it finds itself is clearly a step in the right direction.

In a positive light, however, by striving to be an educational partner, the profession ostensibly is making an investment in student learning rather than in itself as a profession. The American College Personnel Association's *Student Learning Imperative* (1994) and the National Association for Student Personnel Administrator's *Reasonable Expectations* (1995) and *Propositions* (1996) may provide ample testimony to this effect, assuming that they do, in fact, reflect philosophical principle more than professional preservation. As these documents attest, helping to shape the culture in which classroom learning occurs, supporting students in the important and necessary transitions to academic studies, befriending students through both formal and informal contacts, and challenging students to connect out-of-class experiences with in-class theories, experiments, and discussions, positions the student affairs profession—in full cooperation with faculty colleagues—to provide a learning experience that is seamless. Emphasizing collaboration with other learning leaders ultimately may provide a useful counterbalance to the negative effects of a profession bent on professionalization.

What will the next ten years hold for the student affairs profession? At the very least, student affairs associations and practitioners will have to do more than simply say that they are partners in the educational mission of institutions—they will have to demonstrate that they are as well. The profession's graduate training programs will have to change to reflect their interest in such a cause; professional associations will have to adapt their conference programs to emphasize student learning above all else, or connect with other associations that do; professional journals will have to move out of current comfort zones regarding topics and language to incorporate a broader understanding of institutional mission, curriculum, and learning theory; and practitioners will have to design and implement programs for which they can articulate clearly its connection to student learning.

Much work must be done, of course, to bring the practice of the profession into harmony with its rhetoric concerning educational partnership and seamless learning. As Allen and Garb (1993, p. 99) conclude: "It is no longer sufficient to do excellent work within the boundaries of student affairs, as defined by organizational charts." We believe that Christian educators, including Christian student affairs professionals, have much to offer in shaping conversations about the profession's foundations and practice. Although in the past many Christian student affairs professionals followed the lead of their non-Christian counterparts, we suggest that the time has come for Christians in the field to be more proactive in constructing the history of the field that is yet to unfold. Perhaps these chapters will provide some points of departure for such an undertaking.

References

Allen, K. & Garb, E. (1993). Reinventing student affairs: Something old and something new. *NASPA Journal, 30* (2), 93-100.

American College Personnel Association (ACPA). (1975). A student development model for student affairs in tomorrow's higher education. *Journal of College Student Personnel, 16* (4), 334-41.

American College Personnel Association (ACPA). (1994). *The student learning imperative: Implications for student affairs.* Alexandria, VA: ACPA.

Astin, A. (1985). *Achieving educational excellence: A critical assessment of priorities and practices in higher education.* San Francisco: Jossey-Bass.

Astin, A. (1993). *What matters in college: Four critical years revisited.* San Francisco: Jossey-Bass.

Barr, M., Upcraft, M. L., & Associates. (1990). *New futures for student affairs.* San Francisco: Jossey-Bass.

Bloland, P., Stamatakos, L., & Rogers, R. (1994). *Reform in student affairs: A critique of student development.* Greensboro, NC: ERIC Counseling and Student Services Clearinghouse.

Chickering, A. (1969). *Education and identity.* San Francisco: Jossey-Bass.

Chickering, A., & Reisser, L. (1993). *Education and identity* (2d ed.). San Francisco: Jossey-Bass.

Clothier, R. (1931). College personnel principles and functions. In G. Saddlemire and A. Rentz (Eds.). *Student affairs: A profession's heritage* (pp. 9-20). Alexandria, VA: American College Personnel Association.

Council of Student Personnel Associations in Higher Education (COSPA). (1975). Student development services in postsecondary education. *Journal of College Student Personnel, 16,* 524-28.

Cowley, W. (1964). Reflections of a troublesome but hopeful Rip van Winkle. In L. Fitzgerald, W. Johnson, and W. Norris (Eds.), *College student personnel* (pp. 24-32). Boston: Houghton Mifflin Company.

Dalton, J. (1993). Organizational imperatives for implementing the essential values. In R. Young (Ed.), *Identifying and implementing the essential values of the profession* (New Directions for Student Services, no. 61, pp. 87-96). San Francisco: Jossey-Bass.

Davenport, R., Roscoe, B., & Brandell, M. (1995, October). *Eliminating the student affairs division: A strategy to improve student service delivery.* Paper presented at the Williams Midwest-Central Regional Conference of the Academic Affairs Administrators Association, Michigan State University, East Lansing, MI.

Eliot, C. (1869). The new education. *Atlantic Monthly, 23* (February and March), 202-20, 365-66.

Etheridge, R. (1967). The dilemma of professional development: Some points of view. *NASPA Journal, 5* (2), 76-80.

Fley, J. (1979). Student personnel pioneers: Those who developed our profession. *NASPA Journal, 17* (1), 23-31.

Fley, J. (1980). Student personnel pioneers: Those who developed our profession. *NASPA Journal, 17* (3), 25-36.

Garland, P. (1985). *Serving more than students: A critical need for college student personnel services.* Washington, DC: Association for the Study of Higher Education.

Geiger, R. (1986). *To advance knowledge: The growth of American research universities, 1900-1940.* New York: Oxford University Press.

Goodchild, L., & Wechsler, H. (Eds.) (1989). *ASHE reader on the history of higher education.* Needham Heights, MA: Ginn Press.

Harrington, K. (1992). *The history and purpose of higher education.* Unpublished manuscript.

Hofstadter, R. & Smith, W. (Eds.). (1961). American higher education: A documentary history (vol. 2). Chicago: University of Chicago Press.

Horowitz, H. (1987). *Campus life.* Chicago: University of Chicago Press.

Kerr, C. (1991). *The great transformation in higher education, 1960-1980.* Albany, NY: State University of New York Press.

Kerr, C. (1994). *Troubled times for American higher education: The 1990s and beyond.* Albany, NY: State University of New York Press.

Kuh, G., Schuh, J., Whitt, E., & Associates (1991). *Involving colleges: Successful approaches to fostering student learning and development outside the classroom.* San Francisco: Jossey-Bass.

Lloyd-Jones, E. (1949). The beginnings of our profession. In E. Williamson (Ed.), *Trends in student personnel work (pp. 260-64).* Minneapolis: University of Minnesota Press.

Lloyd-Jones, E., & Smith, M. (1954). *Student personnel work as deeper teaching.* New York: Harper & Brothers.

Lloyd-Jones, E. (1968). How to prepare for the unknown. *NASPA Journal,* 6 (1), 24-28.

Marsden, G. (1994). *The soul of the American university.* New York: Oxford University Press.

Marsden, G., & Longfield, B. (Eds.). (1992). *The secularization of the academy.* New York: Oxford University Press.

National Association of Deans and Advisors of Men (NADAM). (1943). *Proceedings: Twenty-fifth annual conference of the National Association of Deans and Advisors of Men.* Columbus, Ohio.

National Association of Student Personnel Administrators (NASPA). (1989). *Points of view.* Washington, DC: NASPA.

National Association of Student Personnel Administrators (NASPA). (1995). *Reasonable expectations.* Washington, DC: NASPA.

National Association of Student Personnel Administrators (NASPA). (1996). *Propositions.* Washington, DC: NASPA.

Noll, M. (1994). *The scandal of the evangelical mind.* Grand Rapids: Eerdmans.

Pascarella, E., & Terenzini, P. (1991). *How college affects students.* San Francisco: Jossey-Bass.

Rhatigan, J. (1978). A corrective look back. In J. Appleton, C. Briggs, and J Rhatigan (Eds.), *Pieces of eight* (pp. 9-41). Portland, OR: NASPA Institute of Research and Development.

Ringenberg, W. (1984). *The Christian college: A history of protestant higher education in America*. St. Paul, MN: Christian University Press.

Rothblatt, S. (1993). The limbs of Osiris: Liberal education in the English-speaking world. In S. Rothblatt and B. Wittrock (Eds.), *The European and American University Since 1800* (pp. 19-73). Cambridge: Cambridge University Press.

Rudolph, F. (1962). *The American college and university: A history*. New York: Vintage Books.

Ryken, L. (1987). Reformation and puritan ideals of education, In J. Carpenter and K. Shipps (Eds.), *Making higher education Christian* (pp. 38-55). Grand Rapids: Eerdmans.

Saddlemire, G., & Rentz, A. (1986). The early years. In G. Saddlemire and A. Rentz (Eds.), *Student affairs: A profession's heritage* (pp. 1-3). Alexandria, VA: American College Personnel Association.

Schetlin, E. (1968). Guidance and student personnel work as reflected by Esther Lloyd-Jones from 1929 to 1966. *Journal of the National Association of Women Deans and Counselors, 31* (3), 97-102.

Schwehn, M. (1993). *Exiles from Eden: Religion and the academic vocation in America*. New York: Oxford University Press.

Task Force on Professional Preparation and Practice. (1991). *The recruitment, preparation, and nurturing of the student affairs professional.* Washington, DC: National Association of Student Personnel Administrators.

Tewksbury, D. (1932). *The founding of American colleges and universities before the Civil War: With particular reference to the religious influences bearing upon the college movement*. New York: Teachers College.

Turner, F. (1968). Echoes of the past. *NASPA Journal, 6* (1), 33-42.

Veysey, L. (1964). *The emergence of the American university*. Chicago: University of Chicago Press.

Wells, R. (1989). *History through the eyes of faith: Western civilization and the kingdom of God.* New York: Harper & Row.

Young, R. (1993a). Examining the history of student affairs through the lens of professional education. *NASPA Journal, 30* (4), 243-51.

Young, R. (Ed.). (1993b). *Identifying and implementing the essential values of the profession.* (New Directions for Student Services, no. 61). San Francisco: Jossey-Bass.

Zaccaria, J. (1968). The behavioral sciences and the identity crisis of student personnel work. *Journal of the National Association of Women Deans and Counselors, 31* (3), 103-105.

Zopfi, K. (1991). The history of the Association of Christians in Student Development (ACSD). *Koinonia,* (Fall), 6.

Chapter 3

Student Learning and Student Affairs

David S. Guthrie

THE FIRST CHAPTER provided an overview of worldviews in general and a Christian worldview in particular. We underscore worldview because we consider it a useful framework for understanding one's perceptions about and existence within the world. In this chapter, we apply a Christian worldview directly to the college experience. More specifically, the purpose of this chapter is fivefold. First, we suggest that the efforts of student affairs practitioners must be viewed within the larger context of student learning. We observe that too many student affairs professionals do not consider their work to be part of a comprehensive project to help students learn.

Second, we identify several underlying principles of student learning. Although we admit that these principles may not be exhaustive, they go significantly further in coming to terms with student learning as a concept when compared to the two treatises recently produced by the two leading professional associations in the student affairs field. Moreover, we also wish to clarify how we make sense of student learning from a Christian point of view. We acknowledge that the principles that we offer may not be altogether unique to a Christian view since we contend that ideas may be derived from other worldviews without doing damage to the integrity or distinctiveness of our own. For example, that the existence of gravity is affirmed by Christian as well as other perspectives does not detract from the coherence or uniqueness of a Christian worldview.

Finally, we offer the development of wisdom as the purpose of student learning. We offer both an explanation of what we mean by wisdom development and an analysis of the symmetrical connection between the purpose (i.e., wisdom development) and the principles of student learning. Agreeing with Bloland, Stamatakos, and Rogers (1994, p. ix) that our profession "may be on the threshold of another redefinition," we offer this chapter as a provocative contribution to the dialog not only for those within the field but also for all of those who currently find their home elsewhere in American academe.

39

Establishing a Context for the Work of Student Affairs Professionals

Making sense of the efforts of student affairs professionals cannot occur in a vacuum. Understanding the larger institutional context in which student affairs professionals perform their roles is a necessary first step (Tierney, 1988); one cannot adequately discuss the work of student affairs professionals without discussing where student affairs professionals work. This larger context shapes how student affairs practitioners define and perform their work and affects the ways in which other institutional participants perceive their efforts.

What is the context, then, in which student affairs professionals do their work? Our response is reducible to two words: student learning. Whether it occurs inside or outside of the classroom, formally or informally, individually or corporately, student learning is the raison d'etre of the college experience. This is not to say that student learning is the exclusive domain of colleges and universities. That student learning is the fundamental focus of undergraduate education simply underscores the idea that college provides both a structured and unstructured environment in which students accomplish what is intended—they learn. Clearly, a college in which learning was neither expected nor occurred is a ridiculous if not impossible concept.

Our point in underscoring student learning as the context in which the work of student affairs professionals occurs is simple. We believe that student learning must be the purpose around which student affairs staff construct and implement their efforts. Residence life programs, student organizations and activities, disciplinary proceedings, orientation programs, volunteer projects—in short, all those initiatives typically administered by student affairs professionals—must have student learning as their goal.

We admit some hesitancy in choosing student learning to describe the overarching context of undergraduate education. Largely due to the ascendancy of the assessment movement and, within the student affairs field itself, the recent drafting of the American College Personnel Association's *Student Learning Imperative* (1994) and the National Association of Student Personnel Administrator's *Reasonable Expectations* (1995), student learning has become an oft-used buzzword in contemporary academe. Notwithstanding its widespread usage, however, we decided to use student learning because it captures both institutional contexts (i.e., the college environment) and individual and group processes (i.e., those involved in the learning process).

From our perspective, student learning also offered the best overall emphasis on the nature of the college experience. That is, we believe that college is more appropriately about student learning than it is about teaching, the mastery of a body of knowledge, personal development, employment credentialing, the discovery of new knowledge, or institutional reputation and resources. Although teaching, knowledge mastery, personal development, and so on most assuredly occur in college, we suggest that they most properly take place within the primary context of student learning (Guskin, 1994a; Guskin, 1994b).

Establishing student learning as the context in which the work of student affairs practitioners occurs is an important starting point in explaining our view. Much more needs to be said, however, with respect to how we understand student learning. This is important in at least two regards. First, despite the recent, relative popularity of student learning as a concept within the field of student affairs, neither the ACPA nor the NASPA documents mentioned above provide much substance regarding its meaning; evidently both treatises assume that the definition of student learning is unequivocal. In contrast, we think it improper to discuss student learning, particularly when we (and "they") identify it as the underlying context of higher education and student affairs, without also elaborating what we mean by the concept. And, second, explaining how we understand student learning is important because, in keeping with the focus of the book, we believe a Christian view of student learning has something valuable to contribute to the conversation. In the section that follows, we discuss several component principles of student learning as a means of indicating how we define student learning.

Principles of Student Learning

Although the principles that follow are manifestations of our Christian beliefs, we believe that their relevance and application is broad. In fact, we suggest that many institutions—Christian and otherwise—may apply these principles in cultivating a particular institutional context for student learning. Stated another way, the principles that follow may take on different meanings based on the particular mission that guides student learning at a particular institution. Even wisdom development, which we describe later in the chapter as the purpose of student learning, may be framed by the distinctive contours of an institution's mission. Ultimately, we hope that institutional participants will consider these principles as they construct their student learning project. We are particularly interested in helping Christian colleges wrestle with these principles as they strive to appropriate student learning initiatives—including those undertaken by student affairs professionals—that are shaped by a Christian worldview.

Student Learning As A Religious Endeavor

Consider the preceding subheading in the form of a question: Is student learning a religious endeavor? Some may readily agree that student learning may *include* religious endeavors. That is, student learning is religious when it involves exposure to religious activities such as a religion class, a dorm Bible study, or an on-campus ecumenical or denominational worship service. Others may agree that some contexts of student learning are more religious than others relative to an institution's mission statement. Proponents of this view, for example, may offer that learning at a church-related college is comparably more of a religious endeavor than it is at a nonsectarian institution.

These responses to the question: Is student learning a religious endeavor? reflect a view—we believe a quite common view—that sees religion as a *part* of life; some *parts* of life are religious and other *parts* are not religious. Translated into a college context, such a view considers particular parts of learning as religious and other parts as not religious. For college student affairs professionals, this view may routinely translate into providing opportunities and activities that address various dimensions of students' lives, some of which are defined as religious (e.g., Bible studies, chapel service, workshop on spiritual gifts) and some of which are defined as not religious (e.g., initiative games, workshop on multiculturalism, a live concert—unless, of course, a religious band is involved).

While recognizing that many may hold the view described above, we offer an alternative answer to the question, Is student learning a religious endeavor? Our response is simply "Yes, student learning is a religious endeavor." Based on the Christian framework that we discussed in the first chapter, we believe that the *entirety* of student learning—the organizing frameworks that support it, the activities that comprise it, the staff who enact it, and the students who live it—at *every* institution is a religious enterprise. Chickering and Associates (1981, pp. 9-10) perhaps stated it most lucidly:

> The question is not whether higher education should be in the business of human engineering and social control. It already is in that business . . . .
> Every college and university, public or private, church-related or not, is in the business of shaping human lives.

Saying that student learning is a religious endeavor means that it is shaped by basic beliefs about life. An institution's learning project is not undertaken neutrally but reflects what Schwehn (1993, p. 94) refers to as "morally directive" principles. These moral directives provide substance, form, and purpose to student learning. Seen in this light, student learning, as well as the intended outcomes of student learning, are reflections of an institution's religious persuasions. For example, the "living community" of St. John's College rests on the conviction that "the best preparation for action is contemplation guided by the reading of the best books known to [its founders]" (Brann, 1992, p. 43). Hutchins' University of Chicago was premised on the credo that: "Education implies teaching. Teaching implies knowledge. Knowledge is truth. The truth is everywhere the same. Hence education should be everywhere the same" (Hutchins, 1967, p. 66). And, for Christian higher education, Lowry (1950, p. 104) offers that it "is not just education plus a set of rules, prescribed courses in the Bible and opportunities for worship.

Christianity is basic. It is normative. It has to do with the essence of life and the whole of life. To compartmentalize it is to imprison it, to nullify it." The point is simply this: The ways in which student learning is enacted is related to the fundamental moorings of an institution that typically are expressed in its mission statement. Coming to terms with the nature of student learning is incomplete without an examination of the underlying institutional values that give direction to it.

Student Learning as a Purposeful Endeavor

All institutions make claims about the impact that they desire to have on student learning (Ewell, 1985). Most often these claims are constructed around the cognitive, affective, and practical competencies (Bowen, 1977; Bloom, 1956) that an institution expects its students to attain. Institutional responses to the following questions are of critical importance in this process: What will college students learn? Why? How will such learning occur? Will we be able to recognize anticipated learning or its absence? How? Without a sense of "what learning is for," virtually any educational program or approach will do. Although this option may appear attractive to learning leaders who are inundated with day-to-day administrivia, who are understaffed, or both, this option lacks the well-reasoned purposefulness that we believe is necessary. Later in this chapter, we will discuss what we consider to be the purpose of student learning. As for now, we simply wish to underscore the importance of establishing intentional goals for student learning.

Institutions, however, do not bear sole responsibility for the purposefulness of student learning. Students themselves obviously play necessary roles as well. In this regard, we suggest that learning is purposeful because it is a legitimate human activity; learning is part of what it means to be fully human. In contrast to those who may posit that college is a necessary evil or temporary aggravation, we believe that learning is not only an inherent quality of personhood but being a college student is also a bona fide calling to be undertaken with great diligence and wonder. Needless to say, some students will neglect to view learning in this light. One of the challenges facing the learning leadership of an institution—Christian or otherwise—may be to create ways of helping students learn about the purposefulness of learning both with respect to the college's intentions for the learning process and for the self-awareness—in the truest sense of the term—of individual students.

The Multidimensionality of Learning

We believe that student learning consists of multiple dimensions. While in college, students have the opportunity to develop intellectual, vocational, communal, and personal competencies and styles (Bloom, 1956; Wolterstorff, 1980; Ratcliff; 1992). Students will not only learn the theories, issues, and applications of various academic disciplines but they will also learn about career options, cultural differences, and decisionmaking. They will learn what constitutes a thoughtful term paper as well as how to compose a resume, nurture a friendship, and if and when to "just say no." The point is simply that learning is a multidimensional experience; it occurs within and among many different contexts of the college experience.

Rather than affirm and substantiate a multidimensional view of learning, we contend that many educators unidimensionalize the learning process, or, as Palmer (1983, p. xi) puts it, "live one-eyed lives" in constructing the learning experience. To be sure, entire theoretical systems of education have been constructed around one specific context of learning (e.g., cognitive, moral, psychosocial). Unidimensional approaches reduce learning to a singular context and then use that context as the absolute standard from which to positivize the learning experience as well as interpret and critique alternative dimensions if, in fact, they acknowledge the salience of other dimensions of learning at all.

We see at least four unidimensional learning approaches, reflecting the four dimensions already mentioned above that are currently operative in academe: the rationalist, the credentialist, the maturationist, and the moralist. According to the rationalist view, learning is ultimately about "the inculcation of a disciplinary orientation in students" (Bergquist, 1992, p. 41). Faculty members often may be the most staunch supporters of this academic perspective, especially when compared to many student affairs professionals and students. This view suggests that college is about helping students acquire knowledge by exposing them to past and present people, events, and ideas. Further, those who hold this perspective often assume that knowledge per se as well as its acquisition are neutral realities; knowledge simply exists and faculty teach it to students who, in turn, become educated and capable of functioning within society (Dressel & Marcus, 1982). The rationalist view is flawed insofar as it reduces learning to intellectual cognition. While student learning in the college context necessarily involves one's mind, we believe that the inadequacy of the rationalist view rests with its tendency to conflate learning and thinking. As the reader will see, we believe that being a college-student learner involves much more than being a college-student thinker; similarly, college cannot be reduced to the classroom context alone.

The credentialist view reduces learning to the anticipated outcome of the college experience—obtaining a good or better job. This perspective defines college-student learning as a necessary means—to be sure, not all bad—to a desired end (i.e., gainful employment). Powell (1971, p. 67) summarizes the credentialist view:

> Currently in higher education, the dominant goal appears to be, not self-development, but rather job accreditation. Tests, grades, honors, degrees—these tangible signs of approval and success form the basis for

what takes place in the classroom, and the students are taught that securing
and achieving them indicate that one is "accredited" and ready to leave the
campus and take a job reserved for those with such credentials.

Although students appear most likely to embrace this view, some institutions
also demonstrate allegiance to it by developing formal curricular programs on
the basis of hot job markets. As the argument goes, an institution's potential
to survive will depend on its ability to identify and offer the programs that its
clients desire, particularly during times of shrinking resources and stable, if
not declining, application pools. From our perspective, the credentialist view
as a stand-alone dimension of learning is also inadequate. Although we applaud
it for its apparent sensitivity to students' vocational needs and interests, we
think it devalues the learning process by placing inordinate emphasis on the
postcollege work experience (Where will I work after I graduate?) rather than
on the in-college experience itself (What can I learn while I'm in college?).

The maturationist view of college-student learning places primary value
on students' personal, wholistic development and is typically championed by
student affairs professionals. According to this view, college is about helping
students develop as whole human beings. This wholistic development, which
is presumed to occur sequentially (i.e., in stages), does not preclude formal
classroom education but places considerable emphasis on what is typically
termed the cocurriculum, the content of which may include developing
competence, managing emotions, moving from autonomy toward
interdependence, developing mature interpersonal relationships, establishing
identity, developing purpose, and developing integrity (Chickering, 1969;
Chickering & Reisser, 1993). Specific "efforts such as career development,
counseling, student activities, living-learning environments, student
government, and leadership training" comprise this "pragmatic" approach
(Knock, Rentz, & Penn, 1989, p. 119). Further, particular topics such as time
management, decisionmaking, alcohol abuse, stereotypes, sexuality, and the
like are often common subject matters in maturationists' syllabi. Although we
acknowledge the importance of these issues and believe that college students
should come to terms with their own understandings and subsequent actions
regarding them, we think the maturationist view of student learning is, by
itself, inadequate. On the surface, the maturationist view seems to
acknowledge multiple contexts for student learning; its use of wholistic
learning appears promising. As it has evolved historically, however,
particularly as it has been embraced and enacted by student affairs
professionals, the maturationist view places ultimate emphasis on individual
human dignity and mutual empowerment (Young, 1993a; Young, 1993b) as
the units of analysis. The result is that maturationists often diminish, or lose
sight of altogether, the particular context in which such development occurs

(i.e., college), as if context is irrelevant to the nature and content of one's development.

The moralist view of learning considers college to be the incubator for students' spiritual coming of age. According to this view, which is perhaps most common at Christian institutions, college empowers students to become more holy or godly by providing an assortment of constraints (e.g., enforced curfew, no movies, dress code, no dancing) and opportunities (e.g., mandatory chapel, substantial curricular requirements in theology/biblical studies) that will appropriately disciple students. We affirm the moralist perspective's interest in developing students' ultimate commitments and practical expressions of Christian faith. The moralist approach to learning, however, tends to redefine college learning as a four-or-five-year worship experience that prepares students for lives of ministry irrespective of particular careers. As such, it blurs the distinction between college and church and ostensibly misses the point of the college experience—student learning.

All of the views above apotheosize a certain dimension of learning to the diminution of other learning contexts: for rationalists, learning is cognition and occurs by exposure to the formal curriculum; for credentialists, learning is the sine qua non to a career; for maturationists, learning is self-improvement and occurs in life experiences, irrespective of specific context; and, for moralists, learning is piety formation in preparation for spiritual service. In contrast to these constricted views of learning, we affirm that learning is multidimensional. We clearly do not mean to insinuate that college-student learning does not involve cognition, have relevance for career goals, contribute to personal development, or perhaps contribute to an increased commitment to one's ultimate concerns. Rather, we simply wish to underscore the idea that the learning that occurs in college is irreducible to a singular component; it consists of various contexts taken together. Moreover, although we argue for a multidimensional understanding of learning, we eschew a view of learning that is a simple sum of fragmented parts. We also affirm that learning must be integrated, and it is to that discussion that we now turn.

Integrated Learning

The notion of integrated learning is not new. During the last decade alone, many voices have denounced the atomization of undergraduate education in which "students are shoppers and professors are merchants of learning" (Association of American Colleges, 1990, p. 66) and decried the importance and benefit of a coherent, unified educational experience. Boyer (1987, p. 92), for example, admonished institutions to consider integrated learning as a precondition for helping students gain a "more authentic view of life."

A Christian view is equally committed to integrated learning. It underscores the idea that the component dimensions of what a college provides its students—both inside and outside the classroom—are mutually connected and shaped by particular expectations for what will occur. Stated another way, we view the entire college experience as if it was a singular course or class. In the same way that a professor might design a classroom course to include objectives; anticipated outcomes; topics to be discussed and their relationships to one another; assignments; and requirements so must the educational leaders of a college construct a coherent course for student learning. This course will necessarily include cognitive, vocational, maturational, and moral challenges; it will involve analyzing ideas, interning for a company or a school, managing time, and exploring values. Most importantly, however, for college to be recognized and experienced as an integrated course requires the interconnectedness of these components. Once again, in the same way that a professor would not frame a classroom course by assembling fourteen weeks worth of unrelated issues, so must those responsible for learning leadership at a college strive for cohesion among various dimensions of the educational experience. This suggests that what a student may learn in a sociology class may not be isolated from her efforts as a leader of a student organization or as a roommate in a residence hall. Similarly, an economics professor's efforts to explain community development may be augmented by requiring students to observe a local neighborhood association or by encouraging students to volunteer at a social-service agency with a friend. In presenting an integrated approach to learning, we simply wish to emphasize that, although multidimensional, learning is best achieved when educational leaders and students alike understand and experience overlap and connection among various contexts of learning (Thomas, 1992).

Understanding integrated learning conceptually is substantially easier than creating and sustaining a college learning experience that embraces it. Of particular relevance to the purpose of this book is the relationship between student affairs and academic affairs divisions viz-à-viz integrated student learning. Many colleges and universities, including Christian institutions, undertake education with what may be referred to as a bipartite strategy. Student affairs professionals offer learning opportunities outside of the classroom and faculty members provide learning opportunities inside the classroom. Some may argue further that one house (academic affairs) is fundamentally more important than the other (student affairs) because the learning with which it concerns itself is of an inherently higher order. After all, as the rationale may go, who would argue that teaching a student to understand Plato's *Allegory of the Cave* is quintessentially more important than helping a student revise an editorial for the college newspaper or debriefing some students after the completion of a low-high ropes course. Before straying too far afield, however, the point we wish to highlight is that many institutions currently operate a system in which student and academic affairs divisions coexist but have relatively little to do with the other (Brown, 1988). Whether the current bifurcated system endures due to the efforts of those perceived to possess relative power (i.e., academics) or to those perceived to wield relatively little power (i.e., student affairs staff), the net effect is unchanged—inside-of-class learning and outside-of-class learning are dichotomous tasks that, though they occur at the same institution, have little in common; indeed, the use of the word division may describe the current organizational reality quite nicely.

The learning that these respective divisions deliver to students is fragmented as well. Academic affairs offers the formal curriculum, student affairs provides the cocurriculum, but formal curriculum and cocurriculum are largely unrelated and subsequently unconnected. Cross (1976, pp. 139-40) is worth quoting at length on this point:

> After all the years spent in academe analyzing the fallacy of various forms of dualism, it is ironic that we should find ourselves practicing cognitive-affective dualism in education. We have created separate (and not quite equal) structures to handle a dualistic conception of education . . . at worst, [this division of labor] depicts an erroneous and even dangerous conception of education in which values and attitudes are considered affective education—as though human values were devoid of intellectual analysis—while the study of physics is considered cognitive education—as though the development of humane and compassionate use of scientific knowledge were irrelevant to its possessor.

The net result of this fragmented approach, at best, is a nonintegrated, two-curriculum college in which students learn a little about this and that but very little about this with that. While some educational leaders may, for principal or pragmatic reasons, find the simple-sum-of-disparate-parts view of learning satisfactory, we contend that such a view of learning is inconsistent within a Christian framework. In contrast to this approach, we believe that a inseparable, reciprocal connection exists between the learning experiences—both inside and outside the classroom—that students have during college. Building on the contexts that we mentioned in the previous multidimensionality section and to illustrate an integrated learning approach, we suggest that a student's intellectual learning cannot be isolated from its connection with her expanding understanding, analysis, and pursuit of vocational calling; personal identity and expression; and moral responsibility. Similarly, we suggest that a student's vocational learning cannot be separated from its connection with his expanding understanding, analysis, and pursuit of ideas and theories; gifts, skills, and experiences; and societal needs and opportunities. And so it goes; each component of learning is connected to and finds expression within every other learning dimension. In the final analysis, a Christian perspective suggests that the desired emphasis of student learning is not on the relative importance of in-class versus out-of-class learning; nor is it on the relative success of an institution to provide as many curricula—formal and informal—as possible from which students can learn. Rather, a Christian view highlights the importance of establishing clear connections among the various learning contexts that students experience in college. Coles (1994, p. A64) is particularly insightful on this point:

> Our colleges and universities could be of great help to students . . . if they tried more consistently and diligently to help students connect their experiences . . . with their academic courses . . . Students need the chance to directly connect books to experience, ideas and introspection to continuing activity—through discussion groups in which the thought and ideas that are so suggestively conveyed in fiction and in essays are brought to bear on the particular individuals who inhabit a world of hardship and pain.

In summary, placing primacy on integrated student learning redefines how we talk about and perform education itself. Emphasizing what Shaffer (1993, p. 166) refers to as the "total educational experience" provides an opportunity to discard the current curriculum/cocurriculum language in favor of a singular, yet multifaceted and unified, curricular experience for students. From our perspective, a college's curriculum not only includes in-class and out-of-class experiences, but also intentional efforts are made to establish connection among all of these experiences in such a way that students learn what the college desires them to learn in accordance with its stated objectives. As a student enters college, then, she begins a journey in which the paths she explores both inside and outside of the classroom offer ample, coherent testimony to the learning outcomes espoused by the institution.

Learning as a Communal Endeavor

Given what we have offered thus far, that we now suggest that student learning is a communal endeavor seems to follow. That is, developing a student-learning project conscientiously, purposefully, and multidimensionally yet with integrality, depends in an inordinate way on the mutual respect and willing collaboration of an institution's educational leadership. Needless to say, establishing and sustaining what Nisbet (1973, p. 229) referred to as "intellectual fellowship . . . with fruitful communication among all levels" is not easy. Some may even suggest that community is an unrealistic goal of the academy because it "call[s] backward to a smaller, simpler world" and may "actually impede efforts to make better that which must be . . ." (Kerr, 1967, p. 7). We suggest, however, that community is the appropriate context for student learning. In the context of self-effacing partnership, student learning ostensibly achieves its intended wonder and celebration rather than drudgery and utility (Long, 1992).

With respect to the participants in student learning, the institutional roles of faculty members and student affairs professionals are redefined when learning is a communal endeavor. The joint responsibility of members of student and academic affairs divisions becomes the pursuit and actualization of intended learning outcomes in their day-to-day work. Seen in this light, student learning "becomes the superordinate value that brings academic and student affairs into complementary balance (Allen & Garb, 1993, p. 98). Members of academic and student affairs divisions alike become members of the same student learning team, united in their efforts to contribute harmoniously to students' college experience. Regardless of their particular appointment within a college, faculty members and student affairs staff members work together toward implementing a cohesive, univocal curriculum—some of which will occur inside the classroom and some of which will occur outside the classroom—that fosters student learning consistent with the institution's intentions for such.

Students themselves also are clearly involved with an institution's learning leadership in the learning process. Although students are perhaps the primary object of a college's student learning project, concluding that they alone are learners or are only learners is mistaken. Rather, other members of the educational community (e.g., faculty and staff members) learn conjointly with students throughout the year. Similarly, students regularly participate in helping others learn regardless of whether the issue is an economic theory, a college committee assignment, or a dating behavior and irrespective of whether the learning comrade is a professor, student, or dean. The fundamental point that we wish to emphasize is that although particular roles may vary, students, faculty, and staff alike are mutually supportive colleagues in student learning.

As one may suspect, the idea of community is a source of great importance within the Christian tradition. As a result, perhaps a biblical metaphor that likens the church universal to a human body comprised of various parts (1 Corinthians 12) may be instructive in illustrating the communal nature of student learning that we espouse. This New Testament passage explains that while a human body has many parts (e.g., head, eyes, hands, feet) that have different functions, in proper relationship, these parts are mutually dependent upon and related to one another in the daily fulfillment of life; human body parts are designed to work together. Similarly, an institution's participants have various tasks to perform to be sure but work collaboratively toward executing the student learning experience. Seen in this light, professors, student affairs practitioners, and students are members of the same body by virtue of their common commitment to student learning and, though they have varied responsibilities for fulfilling this commitment, it is unnatural that they would not function interdependently in the pursuit of a univocal curriculum reflecting institutional goals (Willimon & Naylor, 1995).

Learning as Process Rather Than Goal

The notion that learning is what students "get" in college is a recurring theme in American higher education. From the intentionally prescribed curricula and behavioral standards of the colonial colleges to the specific formulae for "cultural literacy" (Hirsch, 1987), Freire's (1972, p. 58) so-called banking concept has been a popular educational motif. According to this view:

> Students are the depositories and the teacher is the depositer. Instead of communicating the teacher issues communiques and makes deposits which the students patiently receive, memorize, and repeat.

In contrast to this "binge and purge model" (Long, 1992, p. 156) of learning, we prefer to think of learning as what students do, a process in which they actively participate. By emphasizing the process of learning in this section, we do not mean to ignore the value and necessity of content and pedagogy. We simply wish to highlight several of the dynamic human elements that characterize the learning process.

First, the learning process is largely shaped by the learners and their stories. Students enter college having previously experienced classrooms, teachers, tests, studying, student organizations, assignments, grades, books, projects, labs, sports, libraries, and the like. Prior to enrolling in their first college courses, and notwithstanding that their notions may change subtly or substantially, they have already fashioned perceptions about what learning is and how they do it—or don't do it. In addition to prior schooling experiences, students come to college with family histories; socioeconomic statuses; racial, cultural, religious, sexual, and geographic identities; and personal interests, competencies, pathologies, and opinions. Stated another way, learning is an ongoing "bringing to the table" all that one is and engaging new people, ideas, and experiences with a view toward being different than when one began. Understanding that students are nuanced human beings in process is an important component to our view of learning. Needless to say, the comments above are equally true for nonstudent learners as well, namely faculty members and administrators.

Second, we emphasize learning as a process because it may be characterized as exploration and discovery. In the German model of higher education, which gained prominence in America in the nineteenth century, the role of a student was illustrated by the word *lehrenfreheit*, which suggested an insatiable curiosity to uncover truth that, in turn, propelled a student to constant study and investigation. A Christian point of view also offers a compelling rationale for student learning that is rooted in the idea, mentioned earlier in this chapter, that learning is a legitimate human activity. The very nature of this activity is an unfolding process in that a college student explores a variety of ideas, experiences, and activities not only to understand and critique what others have previously discovered but also to fashion a maturing awareness about and commitment to one's fundamental beliefs about things. Seen in this light, the student learning process is likened to a "cat and mouse game" of exploring the "sense and order and meaning to life" (Brueggemann, 1982, p. 13).

For a Christian student, this discovery process may take the form of studying political theory to analyze others' views and practices based on a biblical understanding of civic life and also to construct a political theory that positivizes Christian principles. Similarly, a Christian student who is navigating a relationship with a new roommate may explore various courses, rely on past experiences, personal notions and expressions of friendship, and the approaches of other colleagues all the while in the process of probing what it means to be a good neighbor given a biblical view of life. Although a Christian student is motivated to uncover God's intentions for political theory and personal relationship respectively, in the previous examples, these intentions are not necessarily a priori givens nor are they universally appropriated with respect to time and place. Stated another way, the Christian student's search for God's way in all areas of life is ultimately a reflection of the very nature of the learning process itself.

Third and related to the idea that learning is exploration is the idea that learning is seldom without struggle. In the same way that the exploration of unchartered territory may include surmounting obstacles or even dangers, the learning process may be characterized by strife. Frustration, confusion, and conflict are inevitable in the learning process. A student who is writing a term paper may agonize with how best to translate her own analysis of the subject into thoughtful paragraphs. Another student who is confronted with violating a college's alcohol policy may question the big deal. Another student may feel exasperated in trying to rectify a rift in a significant relationship. Still another student may experience considerable dissonance because his belief system is challenged by the reading assignments, discussions, and service-learning project in an introductory philosophy class. When viewed as a process, learning necessarily involves wrestling and discomfort. As a student engages the ideas, experiences, people, and structures inherent in college life, he or she will be unable to avoid struggle; it is simply endemic to the learning process. On a more positive note, Giroux (1988, p. 128) suggests that this struggle, though difficult at times, is worth enduring because it may result in lives that consider "despair unconvincing and hope practical."

Fourth, and also related to the idea that the idea learning is exploration, is that learning is seldom linear. Once again, in the same way that the exploration of a new world may involve dead ends, backtracking, and wandering, the learning process may be framed as substantially serendipitous. Although developmental-stage theorists may balk at the idea, we contend that student learning is, as Cross (1976, p. 137) puts it, "a bit like the weather," in that student learning fluctuates, seems unpredictable, varies from student to student day-to-day, and is sometimes delightful and sometimes aggravating. That is, rather than move incrementally and in an orderly fashion through ascending developmental stages, as Miller, Winston, and Mendenhall (1983) contend, we believe that the process of learning is most accurately described as students regularly "bouncing around" in and out of various stages; they learn in starts and jolts. As they explore and experiment with the ideas, individuals, and contexts that college offers, many of them, in fact, do make progress toward the higher stages of development, whether it be self-actualized, identity achieved, committed in relativism, principled, internalized, or the like. In short, students learn and colleges help them do so.

Finally, we highlight learning as a process because we affirm that it does not cease on commencement day but extends throughout life. As Springsted (1988, p. 79) suggests: "[College] initiates a quest to know that will continue throughout the rest of one's life." The learning that occurs between new student orientation and graduation—both in-class and out-of-class—functions as an additional resource and context for a student's life that, in turn, contributes to the shaping of his or her life beyond college. Notwithstanding the differential impact that learning during college may have on learning after college, we affirm that learning is a lifelong process characterized by the issues discussed above.

Thus far we have suggested that student learning is the appropriate focus of the college experience and that student learning is a religious endeavor that is purposeful, multidimensional, integrated, communal, and processual. By emphasizing its centrality as well as the principles that we believe characterize it, we do not want to create the impression that student learning is simply an end in itself without goal or direction. Indeed, as we discussed earlier, one of the characteristics of learning is its purposefulness. Therefore, we now turn to a discussion of what we consider the ultimate purpose of student learning.

The Purpose of Student Learning

Almost twenty years ago, Bowen (1977, p. 31) succinctly reiterated a timely question: "What do educators hope will be the results of their efforts?" As we indicated at the outset of the previous section, how individuals enact learning reflects their ultimate belief system. Confessing allegiance to the Christian faith, therefore, must find some expression in how we respond to Bowen's critical question.

In contrast to the unidimensionalized goals discussed earlier in the chapter (rationalist, credentialist, maturationist, and moralist), we contend that the development of wisdom is the ultimate purpose of student learning, regardless of institutional setting. So, what do we mean by developing wisdom? We offer that growing in wisdom consists of establishing and reestablishing connections among three interrelated processes: remembering, discerning, and exploring. We will discuss each in turn, describing the idea itself and then relating it to a general college context. Because we also want to enliven a conversation among our Christian colleagues, we also note how each process may take shape within a Christian college setting in particular.

Remembering

Remembering is the ongoing recalling of the beliefs, ideas, individuals, and experiences that, previous to the current moment, define who we are and why we exist. As such, remembering is a grounding process; remembering establishes or re-establishes one's bearings for living. Ancient Jews often placed a pile of stones at the site where the presence and power of Yahweh was made manifest to them. The rockpiles throughout the land visually reminded the Jews and their offspring (Joshua 4:21-24) of God's abiding sovereignty and of their identity as a delivered people who were to be a blessing to the nations on behalf of the Lord. The stones served as a heuristic to help them understand their present existence in the context of past stories and the overarching Story.

When applied to a general higher education context, we suggest that remembering is a process in which students continuously come to terms with who, what, why, and where they are. As this process unfolds during the college years, students may find, forge, or hone a meaningful and sufficient framework for understanding and orienting their personal and sociocultural lives.

Within a Christian college in particular, this suggests that in-class and out-of-class learning experiences must be replete with rock piles that help students remember their bearings, that remind students that God is the starting point for understanding and experiencing college. These rock piles may take many intentional forms at Christian colleges including chapel programs, core curricular courses, dorm Bible studies, academic and interpersonal advising opportunities, and supportive friendships. Whatever the case, Christian colleges distinguish themselves by nurturing and shaping students' ultimate beliefs such that they become more skillful at appropriating their faith in all areas of life.

Discerning

By discerning we mean the ongoing process of using one's bearings or rememberings to shape the routines of everyday life. As such, discerning may be likened to a sifting process. That is, in the same way that a prospector sifted stream sediments to find gold, a student sifts ideas, experiences, decisions, and so on in an effort to determine what is good or bad, better or worse, right or wrong, wise or foolish, necessary or optional, or what works or doesn't work.

Extending the metaphor further, the metal wires that crisscross to form a miner's sifting device may be viewed as the bearings through which the events of life are processed.

In the context of higher education in general, discernment (discerning) is a critical component of wisdom-focused student learning. As a student experiences the ideas, people, and events that comprise college life, he or she continuously makes sense of it all based on the rememberings that constitute his or her grid of reality. Continuing the image cited above, the student sifts each aspect of the college experience—Plato, campus lectures, last night's date, information superhighways, the Enlightenment, an orchestra performance, an editorial in the campus newspaper, roommate interactions, and so on—to determine if and how it makes sense given the current bearings that provide an interpretive framework for and about his or her reality. At the same time, a student's interpretive framework or grid is maturing, expanding, or achieving a higher level of sophistication as he or she encounters the ideas, people, and experiences that accompany college life; using the illustration above, metal wires are being added, subtracted, and revised on one's sifting device.

As applies to Christian colleges in particular, focusing on discernment suggests that faculty and staff strive with students to make sense of college—the classes, the organizational structures, the relationships, the experiences, the happenings—in the context of a Christian view of reality. Faculty and staff concomitantly work with students to adapt and hone the biblical grid through which they are challenging students to interpret all aspects of the college experience. In short, the learning leadership of Christian colleges help students determine "if there is any word from the Lord" (Jeremiah 37:17) on every in-class and out-of-class component of the educational experience and, if so, how it might be appropriated in the most Christianly faithful manner (Mulligan, 1994).

Exploring

The third and final component of wisdom development is exploring. Combining the continual, dynamic processes of remembering and discernment with the added reality that "all is not known," we use exploration (exploring) to identify quite simply the thoughtful, expectant living of life. Stated another way, exploration refers to enacting one's life, simultaneously acknowledging that one has commitments and heretofore established discernment patterns, but that one has much more to explore. As such, one's lived life is the arena in which rememberings find expression and nuance as discernment is practiced over and over again and as one explores the yet unknown. In turn, the experiences of one's life provide the context in which one's rememberings mature and ossify (become second nature) and one's discernment becomes more sophisticated. In short, the exploration of life shapes and is shaped by one's rememberings and discernments.

Within the higher education setting in general, exploration may be another way of expressing the totality of the college experience. A student comes to college possessing a certain framework with which to understand the world, uses that framework as a starting point to discern the entirety of the college experience, and yet faces a whole new world both in and out of class. Of course, the experiences that college offers students in and of themselves are a means of helping students develop viable frameworks, increase discernment, and come to terms with what is yet to be uncovered.

For the Christian college in particular, this whole process also takes on great significance. In fact, one might say that this process underscores what ultimately differentiates Christian colleges from ones that make no such claim. That is, a Christian college aims to shape student learning in such a way that students establish more firmly rooted biblical moorings, become more adept at interpreting ideas and experiences through these biblical lenses, and develop the sensitivities to accept and further explore with wonderment the "myster[ies] that cannot be too closely shepherded . . . or protested against . . ." (Brueggemann, 1982, p. 71).

In summary, we believe that the ultimate purpose of student learning is the development of wisdom. The interwoven, evolving, and dynamic processes of remembering, discerning, and exploring shape and are shaped by students as they navigate college; they summarize the nature and goal of learning itself. Our particular hope is that Christian institutions be challenged to view student learning as a process in which students come to possess a discerning faithfulness (Brueggeman, 1982) with respect to what they think and do in all areas of their lives.

Wisdom Development and the Principles of Student Learning

It is important to note the relationship of wisdom development to the six principles of student learning that we discussed earlier in this chapter. Since principles and purposes of learning should be complementary and mutually reinforcing, we include these comments to illustrate the symmetry that exists between wisdom development and the principles of student learning.

First, positing that the goal of student learning is wisdom is a direct reflection of our own religious convictions as Christians. From our perspective, a Christian view of student learning seems to point away from rationalist, credentialist, maturationist, and moralist goals and toward a more holistic notion of the *telos* of learning, which we have called wisdom development. Many may in fact have recognized wisdom as a biblical term from the start. As we have argued, however, one need not be Christian to embrace wisdom development as the appropriate purpose of student learning.

The religious convictions of an institution's learning leadership will necessarily shape how wisdom development is defined, providing valuative substance to the nature of rememberings, discernment, and further exploration in the college context.

For those involved in Christian higher education, this means that simply acknowledging wisdom development as the right educational purpose is insufficient. Rather, learner-leaders at Christian institutions must determine how to shape, reshape, and strengthen students' moorings to a biblical worldview; cultivate students' abilities to distinguish the "wheat and tares" of ideas, experiences, and events; and equip students for the glories and glitches of further exploration—as workers, family members, parishioners, citizens, consumers, friends, scholars, and so on—such that God is honored and people and structures are blessed by their lives.

Second, student learning as wisdom development is filled with purpose. Determining that a college's purpose is ultimately about helping students build a framework of understanding, sharpen their discernment, and become more prepared for continued exploration gives a college clear direction and sufficient specificity for measuring student learning outcomes. Similarly, students themselves will enter the college experience realizing that they will be challenged to come to terms with their own rememberings, to connect their basic beliefs with how they think and live, and to develop fundamental "tendencies" (Wolterstorff, 1980) that will undergird how they experience and make meaning of life.

Third, student learning as wisdom development is clearly multidimensional. Expecting that students will incur wisdom, as discussed above, because they attended each class of their college career; because they landed a good job; because they participated in as many activities as possible; or because they attended every chapel program, Bible study, and worship service available is ludicrous. Rather, students will grow in wisdom to the degree that the learning leadership of a college works with them to provide experiences in and out of the classroom that not only reflect institutional intentions for student learning but also pique students' reflection (remembering), evaluation (discernment), and curiosity (exploration).

Fourth, developing wisdom is an integrative enterprise. By its very nature, growing in wisdom necessitates making connections: among past, present, and future; among beliefs, ideas, and actions; among people, experiences, and events; among classroom, student organization, and personal relationships; among reading, thinking, and doing; and among any combination imaginable. In contrast to educational goals that may intentionally or serendipitously atomize and isolate, wisdom development assumes the integrality of student learning and requires constant attention to helping students discover connections within their college experience and beyond.

Fifth, developing wisdom and the communal nature of student learning are correlative concepts. Remembering, discerning, and exploring are most beneficial to the extent that students, faculty, and staff work—and learn—together. Relying on elders, colleagues, and friends—all fellow comrades in the learning process—enriches one's capacity to gain wisdom, whether such relationship comes in the form of conversation, lecture, disagreement, research, association, reproof, or simply common experience.

Finally, wisdom development reflects the process aspect of student learning. Further, forging a framework for understanding and orienting one's life (remembering) is clearly an ongoing process. Likewise, becoming increasingly adept at sifting ideas, actions, and experiences in keeping with one's ultimate beliefs does not occur overnight; nor does developing the capacity for further exploration with expectant uncertainty, yet settled confidence (Brueggemann, 1982). Ultimately a college that is committed to helping students grow in wisdom will convey that gaining wisdom itself is not a destination that will be reached upon graduation but is instead a lifelong process.

Summary

We have identified student learning as the appropriate context of higher education and student affairs. Moreover, we have done so in a way that both contributes more to the conversation than the ACPA and NASPA documents and reflects our Christian point of view. In addition, we offer wisdom development as a rich, nuanced means of framing the purpose of the overall educational experience. As a strategy to extend this conversation, we encourage the learning leadership of all colleges—faculty members, academic affairs personnel and student affairs staff—to consider the following questions in evaluating their respective educational enterprises:

* Are institutional efforts, including those undertaken by student affairs professionals, focused on student learning as the defining context of the college experience?
* Are institutional participants, including student affairs professionals, aware of, and do they subscribe, to the underlying beliefs or values that shape the educational enterprise?
* Is student learning undertaken with purpose, with a sense of being clear regarding anticipated outcomes?
* Is student learning construed as a multidimensional experience?
* To what extent do various dimensions of student learning cohere, reflecting interest in pursuing a univocal, integrated curriculum?
* To what extent is student learning a mutually edifying, communal experience?

* How are the processes of student learning accounted for in the educational project?
* Is the development of wisdom that is in view the ultimate purpose of student learning, particularly as characterized by remembering, discernment, and exploration?

References

Allen, K., & Garb, E. (1993). Reinventing student affairs: Something old and something new. *NASPA Journal, 30* (2), 93-100.

American College Personnel Association (ACPA). (1994). *The student learning imperative: Implications for student affairs.* Alexandria, VA: ACPA.

Association of American Colleges. (1990). The decline and devaluation of the undergraduate degree. In C. Conrad and J. Haworth (Eds.), *Curriculum in transition: Perspectives on the undergraduate experience* (pp. 65-94). Needham Heights, MA: Ginn Press.

Bergquist, W. (1992). *The four cultures of the academy.* San Francisco: Jossey-Bass.

Bloland, P., Stamatakos, L., & Rogers, R. (1994). *Reform in student affairs: A critique of student development.* Greensboro, NC: ERIC Counseling and Student Services Clearinghouse.

Bloom, B. (Ed.). (1956). *Taxonomy of educational objectives, Handbook 1: Cognitive domain.* New York: McKay.

Bowen, H. (1977). *Investment in learning: The individual and social value of American higher education.* San Francisco: Jossey-Bass.

Boyer, E. (1987). *College: The undergraduate experience in America.* New York: Harper & Row.

Brann, E. (1992). St. John's educational policy for "living community." *Change,* September/October, 36-43.

Brown, S. (1988). Approaches to collaboration between academic and student affairs: An overview. *NASPA Journal, 26* (1), 2-7.

Brueggemann, W. (1982). *The creative word: Canon as a model for biblical education.* Philadelphia: Fortress.

Chickering, A. (1969). *Education and identity.* San Francisco: Jossey-Bass.

Chickering, A., & Associates. (1981). *The modern American college: Responding to the new realities of diverse students and a changing society.* San Francisco: Jossey-Bass.

Chickering, A., & Reisser, L. (1993). *Education and identity* (2d ed). San Francisco: Jossey-Bass.

Coles, R. (1994). Putting head and heart on the line. *The Chronicle of Higher Education,* (October 26), A64.

Cross, K. (1976). *Accent on learning: Improving instruction and reshaping the curriculum.* San Francisco: Jossey-Bass.

Dressel, P., & Marcus, D. (1982). *On teaching and learning in college.* San Francisco: Jossey-Bass.

Ewell, P. (1985). Assessment: What's it all about? *Change, 17* (6), 32-36.

Freire, P. (1972). *Pedagogy of the oppressed.* New York: Herder & Herder.

Giroux, H. (1988). *Teachers as intellectuals: Toward a critical pedagogy of learning.* Granby, MA: Bergin and Garvey Publishers.

Guskin, A. (1994a). Reducing student costs and enhancing student learning, Part I: Restructuring the administration. *Change, 26* (4), 22-29.

Guskin, A. (1994b). Reducing student costs and enhancing student learning, Part I: Restructuring the role of faculty. *Change, 26* (5), 16-25.

Hirsch, E. (1987). *Cultural literacy: What every American needs to know.* Boston: Houghton Mifflin.

Hutchins, R. (1967). *The higher learning in America.* New Haven: Yale University Press.

Kerr, C. (1967, May 11). The university and utopia. *Daily Californian,* pp. 7-9.

Knock, G., Rentz, A., & Penn, J. R. (1989). Our philosophical heritage: Significant influences on professional practice and preparation. *NASPA Journal, 27* (2), 116-22.

Long, E., Jr. (1992). *Higher education as a moral enterprise.* Washington, DC: Georgetown University Press.

Lowry, H. (1950). *The mind's adventure: Religion and higher education.* Philadelphia: Westminster.

Miller, T., Winston, R., & Mendenhall, W. (1983). Human development and higher education. In T. Miller, R. Winston, and W. Mendenhall (Eds.), *Administration and leadership in student affairs* (pp. 3-29). Muncie, IN: Accelerated Development Inc.

Mulligan, D. (1994). *Far above rubies: Wisdom in the Christian community.* Marshfield, VT: Messenger.

National Association of Student Personnel Administrators (NASPA). (1994). *Reasonable expectations.* Washington, DC: NASPA.

Nisbet, R. (1973). *The social philosophers: Community and conflict in western thought.* New York: Crowell.

Palmer, P. (1983). *To know as we are known: A spirituality of higher education.* San Francisco: Harper & Row.

Powell, R., Jr. (1971). Student power and educational goals. In H. Hodgkinson and L. Meeth (Eds)., *Power and authority: Transformation of campus governance* (pp. 64-82). San Francisco: Jossey-Bass.

Ratcliff, J. (Ed.). (1992). *Assessment and curriculum reform* (New Directions for Higher Education, no. 80). San Francisco: Jossey-Bass.

Schwehn, M. (1993). *Exiles from Eden: Religion and the academic vocation in America.* New York: Oxford University Press.

Shaffer, (1993). "Whither student personnel work from 1968 to 2018?": A 1993 retrospective. *NASPA Journal, 30* (3), 162-68.

Springsted, E. (1988). *Who will make us wise?: How the churches are failing higher education.* Cambridge, MA: Cowley.

Thomas, D. (1992). Church-related campus culture. In D. Guthrie and R. Noftzger, Jr., (Eds.), *Agendas for church-related colleges and universities* (New Directions for Higher Education, no. 79, pp. 55-63). San Francisco: Jossey-Bass.

Tierney, W. (1988). Organizational culture in higher education. *Journal of Higher Education, 59* (1), 2-21.

Willimon, W., & Naylor, T. (1995). *The abandoned generation: Rethinking higher education.* Grand Rapids: Eerdmans.

Wolterstorff, N. (1980). *Educating for responsible action.* Grand Rapids: Eerdmans.

Young, R. (1993a). Examining the history of student affairs through the lens of professional education. *NASPA Journal, 30* (4), 243-51.

Young, R. (1993b). *Identifying and implementing the essential values of the profession* (New Directions for Student Services, no. 61). San Francisco: Jossey-Bass.

Chapter 4

Christian Higher Education and Christian Student Affairs

David S. Guthrie

AS STATED IN the previous chapter, the principles of student learning and the purpose of student learning that we have offered to this point are ostensibly instructive for more than Christian colleges alone. That is, an institution does not have to be a Christian college to define its religious commitments clearly and, based on them, provide a multidimensional, integrated, communal, process-oriented, wisdom-focused student learning experience. Indeed, some institutions currently do so.

At the same time, we believe that the preceding principles and purpose of student learning resonate with a Christian view of life. That more Christian colleges do not frame student learning according to these principles and purpose is therefore particularly curious. Perhaps it is the case that other Christian perspectives logically permit a student learning enterprise that is unidimensional, fragmented, individualistic, prescribed, and/or in pursuit of outcomes other than the cultivation of wisdom. Or, perhaps it is the case that some Christian colleges have simply struggled to connect Christian assumptions with the educational experience, opting instead for a Christian faith that is "privately engaging, but socially [and educationally] irrelevant" (Guinness, 1983). Whatever the reason, we wish to incite discussion not only about principles of student learning that are based on a Christian view but also about how these principles may be implemented Christianly in Christian colleges. In effect, we want to be more specific regarding how Christian educators may appropriate wisdom-focused student learning in Christian institutions. In this chapter, therefore, we offer several general comments about Christian student learning that may assist Christian colleges in renorming and restructuring (Richardson, 1971; Mohrman, et al., 1989) their student learning projects. We also provide three suggestions that may help guide the efforts of Christian student affairs professionals.

Christian Higher Education

We suggest that learning is a normative activity. By normative we simply
mean that God intended learning as a good process that reflects part of what
it means to function as human beings created *imago dei*. God meant for
humans to learn; God's design was that learning would be a delightful capacity
for humans to possess. Our Christian view pictures God's creating humans to
be wholly good, and part of what made humans so good was that God
provided for them to be learners. We highlight this point because we are aware
that, in some Christian circles, learning may be viewed with considerable
suspicion as an instrument of evil. Those embracing this view may point to
literature that indicates that colleges—even Christian colleges—are secularizing
influences on students (Astin, 1993; Hunter, 1987).

We reject the-more-you-learn-the-less-holy-you-become approach in
favor of the view that God created humans to be learners. We do recognize,
however, that human learning can honor or dishonor God. Because our
Christian view also underscores humans' disregard of God's provisions for
life, we readily acknowledge the effects of such disregard on humans as they
go about learning. Although God created humans to be learners, the result of
human autonomy viz-à-viz God is that why, what, and how they learn may not
conform to God's designs for learning.

The significance of our Christian worldview for student learning is that
unrequited learning is not the final word. Rather, the life and work of Jesus is
the final Word. Jesus' redemptive act recovers humans' ability to learn in ways
that conform to what God initially had in mind when God created humans as
learners. For those involved in a college's learning leadership—both faculty
members and student affairs administrators—who are also committed to a
Christian view of life, the very nature of our efforts becomes that of designing
an integrated curriculum of in- and out-of-class initiatives that will help
students uncover what was envisioned when, with delight, God created them
as learners. Although Christians will never get it completely right, they are
obliged to remember, discern, and explore with diligence and "frolic" (Long,
1992, p. 62).

Although we have attempted to make references in the previous chapter
as to how Christian colleges may interpret the purpose of student learning,
several further observations are warranted. First, given the inherently religious
nature of student learning, Christian colleges should strive to provide student
learning Christianly with respect both to content issues and to organizational
structures. This is simply to underscore the idea that neither the content of
student learning nor the systems that undergird it are neutral. For example, for
a Christian college simply to install the formal curriculum of a state university
as its own is inappropriate. Much care must be taken regarding what, how,
and why various subjects comprise the in-class curriculum of a Christian

institution. Similarly, organizational issues such as conduct codes, faculty reward structures, student discipline procedures, graduation requirements, and the like should be intentional, thoughtful byproducts of the Christian beliefs that guide a Christian college. This is not to say that good ideas about student learning—ideas that are consistent with a Christian view of reality—are the exclusive domain of Christian educators. To be sure, many who are not Christian believers have ideas about student learning that are Christian if you will—that is, they make sense within a Christian worldview. Our point here is simply to highlight that the learning leadership of Christian colleges must work to produce and sustain student learning projects for which they can make apology based on their Christian perspective.

Second, Christian colleges must take care to promote multidimensional student learning. Christian colleges, to our mind, must not merely be colleges with chapel programs, theology departments, and dorm Bible studies; likewise, they must not merely be church camps where students also have to read some books and take several tests before departing. Each aspect of the student learning experience—whether cognitive, psychosocial, vocational, or moral—not only must find proper expression in the Christian college but also must be accepted and honored as a legitimate component of student learning by the institution's learning leadership.

Third, a univocal student learning experience should be a hallmark of Christian college education. At a time in which many colleges and universities lack educational coherence—both intradivisionally as well as interdivisionally—Christian colleges can distinguish themselves by providing student learning experiences that hold together. In-class and out-of-class learning coordination must not only occur in Christian colleges but these respective programs must also be complementary. Moreover, perhaps the time has come to discard the traditional organizational structures—academic division and student life division—in favor of a unified, collaborative student learning division in which both those who perform the majority of their work inside the classroom and those who perform the majority of their work outside of the classroom collaborate willingly and enthusiastically as a matter of course (Brown, 1990).

Fourth, there is no room for self-aggrandizing autonomy in the Christian college. The professor who is solely interested in her work, the student whose only concern is his career, and the student life professional who makes no effort to enjoin his faculty colleagues are misfits in a Christian college; for, at the Christian college, an understanding of the community aspect of student learning should enjoy its richest expression. This is not to say that Christian college faculty, staff, and students cannot perform tasks individually or must always act like one big happy family. We simply wish to emphasize that, by virtue of the fact that Christians ultimately view one another as image bearers of God, they enter the learning project with a particular obligation to view and embrace others as valuable contributors to their learning and vice versa.

Finally, Christian colleges may do well to view student learning as part of the process of sanctification. Learning is surely a process. At a Christian college, however, the student learning process takes on a particular significance. There students are introduced to ideas, people, experiences, events and the like, such that they will begin to develop ways of thinking, acting, questioning, and living that are, in the truest sense of the term, godly. This is what wisdom development is all about from a Christian point of view. Willimon (1995, p. 55) offers:

> We are not calling [students] back to something they have previously known but have now forgotten; we are not attempting to open up the closed-minded provincialism of their childhood years; we are not providing cautious Christian nurture for youth who, having been raised in a Christian culture, now need a little spiritual nudge to cultivate the best that is within them. We are taking people to places they have never been, calling them to become part of a countercultural adventure called discipleship, showing them how to perceive the world through a startling perspective called the gospel and adopting them into a new home called the church.

Stated another way, student learning at a Christian college takes shape around the process of students' further developing frameworks of understanding that not only will be sufficient for orienting their lives but will enable them to engage life for life in a way that will honor God (Garber, 1994). As such, attending a Christian college may contribute to one's sanctification, particularly in the realms of thinking Christianly and in faithfully relating what one learns to what one does.

The Marks of Christian Student Learning

One of the principal questions that we frequently returned to in this project was: "How might student learning look if it was done right from our [Christian] point of view?" We were particularly admonished to address this issue in response to Boyer's (1990, p. 283) thoughtful comments:

> At a time in life when values should be shaped and personal priorities sharply probed, what a tragedy it would be if the most deeply felt issues, the most haunting questions, the most creative moments were pushed to the fringes of our institutional life. What a monumental mistake it would be if students, during the undergraduate years, remained trapped within the organizational grooves and narrow routines to which the academic world sometimes seems excessively devoted.

Therefore, we thought it fitting to relay brief "signs and traces" (Adelman, 1989) of Christian student learning that emerged in our conversations. Some of us preferred to think of student learning that is Christianly enacted as making connections, of linking learning and experience, knowing and doing, thought and deed (Hutchingsd & Wutzdorff, 1988; Kolb, 1984). Others liked the idea of learning, made popular by Bellah et al. (1985; 1987), as that which resists "the gravitational pull of privatization" (Palmer, 1990, p. 148) and hones commitment, engagement, and service to other persons as well as to public life. Others championed a biblical notion of maturity as an identifying mark of Christian student learning, meaning that educators assist students in developing into the persons—cognitively, emotionally, relationally, culturally, and so on—that God intends them to be. Still others spoke of right learning as that which inspires students to love or care for those things that God loves or cares for (Holmes, 1991), borrowing from Postman's (1993) recent idea that proper education develops "loving resistance fighters."

The common, identifiable strain that seemed to echo loudly among us was that Christian higher education is about enlivening and equipping students to participate in a "restoration project" (Plantinga, 1990, p. 3). This restoration project involves preparing students with the knowledge, skills, and tendencies (Wolterstorff, 1980) that are necessary in framing and living their personal and civic lives in ways that reflect their ultimate commitments to God. In this sense, college is "a staging ground for action" since the goal is to help students make connections between "what they learn and how they [will] live" (Boyer, 1990, p. 54), such that God may be pleased by their efforts. Perhaps Brueggemann (1982, p. 89) sums it up best when he states: "Education consists in teaching our young to sing doxologies" to God for and in all areas of our earthly lives.

Christian Student Affairs

Student affairs professionals at Christian colleges face many of the same issues and pressures (e.g., marginalization, partnership in student learning) that confront their counterparts at nonsectarian institutions. In addition, they wrestle with how their Christian faith comes to bear in day-to-day practice. In this section, we suggest three guidelines to assist Christian student affairs professionals in their efforts.

Student Affairs as Legitimate Vocation

From a Christian point of view, work of all kinds is legitimate activity. That is, God intends humans to labor in various and sundry tasks—including the student affairs profession. In contrast to those who may consider work a necessary evil, a Christian perspective suggests that humans are commanded to imitate God by laboring creatively as nurses, plumbers, residence hall

directors, pastors, accountants, and so on. Realizing that God calls persons to
their tasks provides a significant and compelling rationale for Christians who
are involved in student affairs roles to consider their work as eminently
purposeful.

In addition, because God has imbued work with such purpose, Christians
employed as student affairs professionals do their work "on purpose." They
do their work intentionally, freely admitting that they possess an agenda.
Working with college students for God's sake, if you will, demands that the
planning and executing of their work be accomplished with particular goals or
outcomes in view; not just any goals or outcomes will do. Creating student
affairs functions and programs for their own sake is inappropriate. While such
an approach may keep student affairs professionals busy, it ignores the
religious nature of their work. That is, Christian student affairs practitioners
must consider as their unique task exploring and uncovering goals and
practices of work—for residence life initiatives, disciplinary procedures,
orientation programs, personal and career counseling, and so on—that reflect
their allegiance to a Christian view of reality. Although we acknowledge that
aspects of various educational theories and programs may resonate with
biblical principles, it should never be the custom of Christian student affairs
professionals to imitate contemporary thinking and practice without serious
reflection and analysis from a Christian point of view. Moreover, as we stated
earlier, perhaps a Christian view of student learning necessitates moving away
from rote fulfillment of the typical functions of the profession in favor of
investigating more integrated approaches to organizing and executing student
learning initiatives and procedures while not ignoring particular tasks that still
must occur.

Student Affairs As Contextualized Endeavor
    At the outset of the previous chapter, we stated that the work of student
affairs practitioners must be viewed in the context of student learning and,
subsequently, went on to explain what we mean by student learning. We now
reiterate this vital point for student affairs professionals in Christian colleges.
The efforts of student affairs staff in a Christian college must occur within the
framework of wisdom-focused student learning that is shaped by a Christian
view of reality. This has several important ramifications for those employed
as student affairs professionals at Christian colleges. First, their job is to help
students learn. We recognize that this view may conflict with the current self-
emphasis of some Christian student affairs professionals as well as the present
roles that others within the Christian academy typically ascribe to them. We
contend, however, that although their efforts most often occur outside the
classroom, the programs, interventions, role modeling, and services that
student affairs professionals at Christian institutions provide must be
educational. Moreover, since education is never undertaken neutrally, the

learning opportunities that student affairs practitioners at Christian colleges offer must also reflect their religious commitments as Christians. Dalton (1993, p. 88) summarizes this underlying principle succinctly:

> The central issue for student affairs leaders, therefore, is not **whether** they should advocate certain essential values but **which** values should be advocated and **how** these values can be advocated in a clear and intentional manner [emphases his].

Because student learning takes shape around the ultimate beliefs of individuals and institutions, it is incumbent upon student affairs professionals at Christian colleges not only to view and enact their work as contributing to student learning but also to do so in ways consistent with their Christian beliefs.

A second consideration, related to the first, is that student affairs professionals at Christian colleges must help students develop wisdom that corresponds with a Christian view of life. The idea that wisdom is the goal of student learning is as important to student affairs professionals as it is to faculty members. Our impression is that some believe professors to be the wisdom producers and student affairs staff to be the trouble preventers; the notion that faculty members are the real educators and student affairs personnel are simply buddies (or bullies) persists, regardless of institutional values. We prefer to think of both faculty members and student affairs professionals as "wise friends" (Willimon, 1993, p. 1018) who help students develop wisdom. As regards student affairs practitioners in Christian institutions, we suggest a strengthened resolve to frame their efforts as those who are assisting students become more wise in conformity to Christian intentions for such wisdom, irrespective of whether these efforts occur in a residence life program, discipline hearing, service-learning project, dining hall conversation, diversity seminar, or movie discussion.

Third, student affairs at Christian colleges should be multidimensional. We sense that student affairs professionals at Christian colleges may tend to construe their efforts as ministry. That is, they provide Bible studies, hymn sings, prayer groups, missions excursions, fellowship groups, volunteer programs, moral encouragement and correction, and servant role modelling. While we do not deny the appropriateness of these endeavors, it is mistaken to believe that this is what constitutes and distinguishes student affairs at Christian colleges. In contrast to this approach, we believe that student affairs practitioners at Christian colleges must be fully engaged in helping students come to terms with emotional, physical, relational, cognitive, vocational, civic, ecclesiastical, aesthetic, and moral issues—in short, with life—from a Christian point of view. What distinguishes student affairs at Christian colleges is not limiting the scope of out-of-class programs to those determined to be decidedly spiritual, but is rather providing multidimensionalized out-of-class initiatives for and with students, all of which are interpreted through a Christian lens.

Fourth, student affairs professionals at Christian colleges must help students make connections among classroom lectures, out-of-classroom involvements, and personal choices. As such, they function as integrators of students' learning experiences (Garland & Grace, 1993)—they help students weld lectures on biomedical ethics with an internship experience in a local hospital; they encourage students to connect service learning experiences with vocational decisions; they assist students in making sense of individual giftedness and choice of major; they challenge students to apply principles of journalism garnered in class to the production of a campus weekly; and the list goes on. This connecting of knowing and doing, this integrating of the components that comprise student learning in college simply makes sense within a Christian view of education. And, although we believe that faculty members at Christian institutions should also assist students in establishing such connections, student affairs practitioners may play a critical role in this endeavor by virtue of their frequent, informal contact with students.

This leads us to a fifth consideration for student affairs professionals at Christian colleges, namely that they should exploit ways to foster a coherent, univocal curriculum with other institutional colleagues, particularly faculty members. This means that student affairs practitioners and faculty members should not only communicate regularly regarding their respective efforts, but should also plan and enact learning initiatives—both in-class and out-of-class—conjointly, involve each other in consulting and strategizing, collaborate on research projects pertinent to student learning, and exhort one another to do their work as to the Lord and on behalf of students. Among professionals in the field writ large, Christian student affairs staff should understand the necessity, importance, and benefit of a communal approach to wisdom-focused student learning. As a result, rather than perpetuate—by design or default—a noncommunal educational approach, student affairs professionals at Christian colleges must press the issue of communally achieved coherent learning.

Finally, Christian student affairs professionals must understand the incompleteness of their efforts. Realizing that learning is processual, that growing in wisdom is a lifelong undertaking, and that helping students become biblically wise thinkers and doers does not eventuate after four years of undergraduate learning may be readily admitted but not nearly so easily accepted. After all, student affairs educators—including and perhaps especially those who are Christian—earnestly desire to believe that their theories of adolescent development are salient, that their educational programs work, and that their interventions and modelling produce appropriate effects. And they do—sometimes, partially, and with some students more than others. Consequently, Christian student affairs professionals do well to accept the limitations of the various educational techniques that comprise their efforts and the naturalness and complexity of the already-but-not-yetness of the learning process as it unfolds unevenly, perhaps in fits and starts, in students' college experiences.

Student Affairs as Ordinary Service

In our zeal to challenge student affairs professionals at Christian colleges to define and shape their work in the context of wisdom-focused student learning that is based on Christian moorings, we do not want to minimize the importance of understanding student affairs as ordinary service. After all the dust settles in the thoughtful pursuit of student learning initiatives that reflect their biblical commitments, Christian student affairs professionals must continue to distribute room keys, help students pack and unpack, and provide them with seemingly mundane, if not trivial, information about drop-add deadlines, linen pick-up, quiet hours, and student-organization reimbursement procedures. We suggest that these tasks and others like them are not insignificant undertakings. Rather, student affairs staff at Christian colleges must view them as opportunities to fulfill their callings not only as professionals but as humble servants of God and persons as well. In the effort to help students learn and grow in wisdom in ways that conform to biblical patterns, student affairs practitioners at Christian colleges must not neglect their obligation simply to serve students.

Conclusion

That some colleges and student affairs professionals do not emphasize student learning, are not consciously aware of or are self-deceived by their ultimate commitments, pay scant attention to connecting beliefs and practices, and function with more than one curriculum are all readily apparent observations. To these realities, however, we add one more: students learn in college. In fact, through both in-class and out-of-class experiences, they may learn that college is not about learning; they may learn that college is not about coming to terms with their own beliefs, commitments, and perspectives—Christian or otherwise; they may learn that institutional mission statements are virtually irrelevant to institutional learning practices; and, they may learn that academic affairs and student affairs divisions have competing agendas. We wish that such learning did not occur; we particularly lament that learning of this sort occurs on Christian college campuses. Perhaps it is precisely because students may learn in these ways that our work as Christian educators is imbued with such critical importance—namely, to offer an alternative way to experience learning in formal classrooms, through student affairs initiatives, and in college coffee shops. To that end, we hope that, in some small way, this book will engage Christian colleges and Christian student affairs practitioners (and perhaps other colleges and student affairs staff), to champion student learning as their primary concern, and to create a coherent, univocal curriculum of wisdom-focused student learning that is the intentional byproduct of their fundamental [Christian] beliefs about life. Then, perhaps the hope expressed so clearly by Long (1992, p. 221) may become more manifest:

> Learning belongs to the leavening and sensitizing dimensions of public life. It is at its best when it enlarges horizons, magnifies the capacity for empathy, commends the importance of dialog, and recommits us to search for life in working viability with others and with an awareness of that which individuals and groups experience as the ground for their most essential being. The importance of practicing the life of learning in that way in the company of a committed guild will never be outdated.

References

Adelman, C. (Ed.). (1989). *Signs and traces: Model indicators of college student learning in the disciplines.* Washington, DC: U.S. Department of Education.

Astin, A. (1993). *What matters in college: Four critical years revisited.* San Francisco: Jossey-Bass.

Bellah, R., Madsen, R., Sullivan, W., Swidler, A. & Tipton, S. (1985). *Habits of the heart.* New York: Harper & Row.

Bellah, R., Madsen, R., Sullivan, W., Swidler, A. & Tipton, S. (1987). *Individualism and commitment in American life.* New York: Harper & Row.

Boyer, E. (1990). *Campus life: In search of community.* Princeton, NJ: Carnegie Foundation for the Advancement of Teaching.

Brown, S. (1990). Strengthening ties to academic affairs. In M. Barr and L. Upcraft (Eds.), *New futures for student affairs: Building a vision for professional leadership and practice* (pp. 239-69). San Francisco: Jossey-Bass.

Brueggemann, W. (1982). *The creative word: Canon as a model for biblical education.* Philadelphia: Fortress.

Dalton, J. (1993). Organizational imperatives for implementing the essential values. In R. Young (Ed.), *Identifying and implementing the essential values of the profession* (New Directions for Student Services, no. 61, (pp. 87-96). San Francisco: Jossey-Bass.

Garber, S. (1994). *Learning to care: The transformation of higher education.* Unpublished manuscript.

Garland, P., & Grace, T. (1993). *New perspectives for student affairs professionals: Evolving realities, responsibilities and roles.* (ASHE-ERIC Higher Education Report, No. 7). Washington, DC: George Washington University, School of Education and Human Development.

Guinness, O. (1983). *The gravedigger file.* Downers Grove: InterVarsity Press.

Holmes, A. (1991). *Shaping character: Moral education in the Christian college*. Grand Rapids: Eerdmans.

Hunter, J. (1987). *Evangelicalism: The coming generation*. Chicago: University of Chicago Press.

Hutchings, P., & Wutzdorff, A. (Eds.). (1988). *Knowing and doing: Learning through experience* (New Directions for Teaching and Learning, no. 35). San Francisco: Jossey-Bass.

Kolb, D. (1984). *Experiential learning: Experience as the source of learning and development*. Englewood Cliffs, NJ: Prentice-Hall.

Long, E., Jr. (1992). *Higher education as a moral enterprise*. Washington, DC: Georgetown University Press.

Mohrman, A., Jr., Mohrman, S., Ledford G., Jr., Cummings, T., & Lawler, E., III. (1989). *Large-scale organizational change*. San Francisco: Jossey-Bass.

Palmer, P. (1990). "All the way down:" A spirituality of public life. In Palmer, P., Wheeler, B., and Fowler, J. (Eds.), *Caring for the commonweal: Education for religious and public life (pp. 147-63)*. Macon, GA: Mercer University Press.

Plantinga, C. (1990, March 6). *Educating for shalom*. Paper presented at a meditation for freshman honors students, Calvin College, Grand Rapids, MI.

Postman, N. (1992). *Technopoly: The surrender of culture to technology*. New York: Knopf.

Richardson, R., Jr. (1971). Comment by Richard C. Richardson, Jr. (In response to article by B. Clark, Belief and loyalty in college organization). *Journal of Higher 42*(6), 516-20.

Willimon, W. (1993). Reaching and teaching the abandoned generation. *Christian Century*, (October 20), 1016-1019.

Willimon, W. (1995). Desperately seeking roots. *Christian Ministry*, (March/April), 55.

Wolterstorff, N. (1980). *Educating for responsible action.* Grand Rapids: William B. Eerdmans.

Chapter 5

Theorizing in Student Affairs from a Christian Perspective

Jeanette Bult De Jong

MOST STUDENT AFFAIRS practitioners today—Christian and non-Christian alike—are aware of various theories that have relevance to their work with college students. The nature of this awareness may differ, however, with respect to their breadth of theoretical knowledge, their perceptions about the usefulness of theory, or their skill in relating theory to practice for the benefit of student learning. To varying degrees, these differences may derive from one's distance from the graduate-school experience, one's personal interest (or lack thereof) in theoretical knowledge per se, one's work demands, or the relative importance of theory within the culture of an institution or student affairs division.

We include this chapter in an effort to expand student affairs professionals' awareness of the role of theory from a Christian perspective. More specifically, we provide a brief overview of the emergence of theory building within the field of student affairs. We also discuss the relationship between a Christian worldview and theorizing, presenting both an endorsement for and a caution about theorizing. Finally, we present a transcribed discussion on Chickering's (1969; Chickering & Associates, 1981; Chickering & Reisser, 1993) theory that occurred among study group members. We include our discussion with the hope that it offers a heuristic of how student affairs professionals might approach theorizing from a Christian point of view.

An Historical Overview of Theory-Building in Student Affairs

Although in loco parentis may be the "original theory of student development" (Upcraft & Barr, 1990, p. 41), extending from the colonial period through the mid-twentieth century, it is perhaps more conventional to state that student affairs is a relatively new field for theoretical inquiry. Notwithstanding drafts of the Student Personnel Point of View (NASPA, 1989) that inaugurated a guiding philosophy for the nascent field by offering some basic assumptions about college students' development, it was not until considerably later that the field adopted more sophisticated theoretical foundations. For example, as late as 1964, one critic leveled the charge that "student activities [personnel] possesses neither an adequate general theory nor adequate `intermediate' theories. To put it jocularly, its philosophy is like a pair of steer horns—a point here, a point there, and a lot of bull in between" (Stroup, 1964, p. 2).

The relative theorylessness of student affairs, however, began to change in the early 1960s. Foundational psychological studies on client centered counseling (Rogers, 1951; 1961) and adolescent development (Erikson, 1950; Piaget, 1964) as well as the contributions of what Upcraft and Moore (1990, p. 44) refer to as "the vocational guidance movement" set the stage for the emergence of more specific and sophisticated theorizing about college students' development. Perhaps the most significant work to launch a theoretical grounding for the student development profession was *The American College*, edited by Nevitt Sanford and published in 1962. In this landmark study, the authors declared higher education a legitimate and ripe field for scientific inquiry and challenged those who would follow to develop more sophisticated theoretical understandings of late adolescent development. Based on this comprehensive anthology, Sanford (1967) later explained the concepts of challenge and support as the twin pillars of student affairs work that appropriately address students' development during the college years.

Sanford's work, in its own right, continues to have relevance today, but his efforts also helped to produce theoretical legitimation for the heretofore inchoate student affairs profession. By the mid-1970s, Perry's (1968) intellectual and ethical development theories, Chickering's (1969) seven vectors of development theory, Kohlberg's (1969) moral development theory, and Loevinger's (1976) ego development theory emerged as essential building blocks for the nascent "student development perspective," and remain so today.

College students themselves, however, were not the only unit of analysis as the field's theory base expanded. Campus ecology perspectives also captured the attention of researchers, as they focused on the dynamic interplay between students and their collegiate environments (Upcraft, 1984). Based on Feldman and Newcomb's (1969) seminal work in this area through the most recent comprehensive tome by Pascarella and Terenzini (1991), these social scientists have made significant theoretical contributions regarding the profound impact of campus environments on students' development.

The theoretical moorings of college student development by the early 1980s were considerably established and propelled professionals in the field to view their work as the development of the student as a person, taking into account both individual and contextual [environmental] factors (Chickering, 1981; Chickering & Reisser 1993; Miller, Winston, & Mendenhall, 1993). Over the course of the last decade, contemporary student development theory cultivated greater sophistication and diversity by building on this central theme. For example, during this time, Astin's (1985) educational involvement theory became a predominant motif for many colleges and universities. Retention theory (Noel, Levitz, & Saluri, 1985; Tinto, 1987), which is rooted in sociological understandings of individuals' rites of passage (Van Gennep, 1966), as well as "mattering" theory (Schlossberg, Lynch, & Chickering, 1989), built on existing developmental and environmental frameworks to clarify the factors that affect student success. In addition, theories that more completely accounted for differences among students regarding gender (Gilligan, 1982), ethnicity (W. Cross, 1978; Wright, 1984; Helms, 1984; Tatum, 1992), age (K. Cross, 1981; Copland, 1989), spirituality (Parks, 1986; Fowler, 1981), and sexual orientation (Cass, 1979) have emerged and continue to receive rapt attention. Student affairs practices that reflect the theoretical maturation of the field have proliferated as well as have institutions that have reconceptualized residential living, diversified student organizations, increased and broadened student program options, added orientation programs, created freshman year experiences, developed cocurricular leadership offerings, and inaugurated initiatives to enhance the collegiate experience for people of color, returning adults, students with disabilities, gay and lesbian students, and women.

Notwithstanding noteworthy expansion and valuable contributions of student development theories during the last three decades, those in the field who are guided by a Christian worldview, by and large, have remained absent from the conversations. Not only has a recognizably Christian theory of students' development not emerged but professional journals on students' development in Christian perspective are also nonexistent. Moreover, although a number of Christian professional organizations exist, they are assembled by denominational affiliation and have little, if any, exchange of ideas among them. The one nondenominational professional organization that does exist—the Association for Christians in Student Development—focuses its [important] efforts on collegiality and networking rather than on theory building and critique and program development. In addition, since only a handful of institutions offer graduate degrees in Christian higher education, most student affairs professionals continue to be educated in graduate programs in which a Christian perspective of life or work is a curious phenomenon at best.

Given this scenario, a compelling rationale emerged for beginning a conversation about students' development in general and student development theories in particular, both of which emanate from our deepest [Christian] convictions about reality. This chapter reflects our effort to provide for

Christians and non-Christians alike a brief look into how those committed to
a Christian worldview may approach theorizing about college students.

Theory as Legitimate Human Endeavor

Most of us dabble with elementary theorizing almost every day, often without
recognizing it as such. For example, a person may notice that after eating
certain foods indigestion or headaches always follow. This simple observation
is the result of the person's establishing a plausible relationship between
behavior (the food that she eats) and experience (the indigestion or headache
that she experiences). Further, the person may test her explanation by avoiding
the culprit foods. If the indigestion or headaches do not recur, most likely the
person will alter her eating habits—at least if she wishes to avoid indigestion
or headaches.

   This illustration identifies the basic ingredients of theorizing. Theorizing
is essentially one's attempt to make sense of the world; theories are
descriptions or word pictures of reality. A theory begins with a hypothesis or
"a guess that is proposed in order to explain something" (Clouser, 1991, p.
52). As such, the hypothesis is typically presented as a tentative
approximation, simplification, or "promising first step" (Suppe, 1977, p. 711)
of what one believes as true or real. As a theorist tests these guesses, a more
detailed and more fully articulated picture gradually emerges, either in support
of or in conflict with the initial hypothesis. Based on the scientist's
work—observation, experimentation, hypothesization, argumentation,
evaluation, modification, correction, and repetition—a theory emerges that
offers an explanation of some aspect of the world in which we live. Stated
most simply, a theorist tries to understand the world by systematically
uncovering and shaping possible explanations about it.

   The history of humanity may be characterized as civilizations' past and
present theorizing or attempting to make sense of the world and their presence
within it. Clearly, our ancestors offered numerous and continuous guesses
regarding the nature of reality, and tested these beliefs with more or less
scientific sophistication. Discoveries throughout the centuries about air, water,
fire, earth, sound, light, plants, animals, and humans combine to provide us
with a massive volume of knowledge that we currently accept as meaningful
explanations about the way things are. From our perspective, it is appropriate
to conclude that theorizing is a natural and fundamental aspect of being
human. And, we have a theory of why this is the case.

   Theorizing is common and prevalent among humans because we believe
that God created people to be meaning seekers. That is, from a Christian
perspective, part of what it means to be human is to explore, discover, and
explain the created order. Embedded in God's command to cultivate and care
for the created order (which we have referred to elsewhere in this book) is the

work of theorizing, of making guesses about the nature of the various, multifaceted aspects of created reality such that character, purpose, and truthfulness are uncovered in ways that are fulfilling to humans and honoring to the Creator. In short, theorizing is a legitimate human endeavor because it is rooted in God's intentions for being fully human.

We think it necessary to underscore the intrinsic value of theorizing that is rooted in the creation account because we are aware that, in some Christian circles, scientific inquiry qua scientific inquiry may be judged a secular endeavor. Although we readily acknowledge that the purposes, methods, or results of some theorizing are in conflict with Christian principles, we think it irresponsible to discard the relationship between theorizing and being human that was established by the cultural mandate (Genesis 1:26-31). Later in this chapter we will caution Christian student affairs professionals not to accept theory blindly; after all, it is one thing to say that theory is a legitimate human endeavor established for humans by God, but it is quite another thing to conclude that all theorizing is good in God's eyes. For now, however, we turn our attention to the importance of theory in the student affairs profession.

The Importance of Theory in Student Affairs

Although student affairs practitioners may quickly acknowledge the importance of theory for their work, we sense that some professionals' day-to-day activities reflect a virtual nonaffirmation of theory and its potential import. For these individuals—Christian and non-Christian alike—theories regarding college students' development are, in effect, inconsequential. Consider several possible points of view.

"Theory is unimportant because there is insufficient time to consider it otherwise."

Although they probably admit the existence of relevant theory, studied it in graduate school, and occasionally make a passing reference to a theorist, some student affairs practitioners are overwhelmed with time demands as they struggle to keep their to-do lists manageable and resist slipping into a tyranny-of-the-urgent mode. Perhaps their lament is understandable: with so much to do, who has the time to keep up with theories and their potential applications. Moreover, as practitioners, student affairs professionals often gravitate toward the practical rather than the theoretical. That is, they frequently rely on intuition or borrow others' ideas when designing programs or developing policy statements. When combined with the press of time, going with gut feelings or mimicking another institution's approach are considerably more expedient than reviewing the literature on theory-based initiatives and their scientifically assessed developmental outcomes.

"Theory is unimportant because acceptance and performance in the field is often independent of a theoretical knowledge base."

Even though many student affairs position descriptions list "working knowledge of the theory base of student development" as a required qualification, it is often compromised in the face of what is judged to be more critical or desirable qualifications. The diversity of functions within the broad field of student affairs (residence life, judicial affairs, student activities, service-learning, spiritual activities, career services, counseling, alcohol education, leadership development, health services, and so on) requires an equally varied skill set in the people leading these departments or offices. It is often assumed, for pragmatic reasons, that if a candidate has the right skill set and most of the qualifications, he or she can pick up the knowledge base while on the job. Whether or not he or she actually does have these qualifications usually does not determine his or her success or failure. The best practitioners do not necessarily possess the best track record in applied theory; conversely, those who have mastered the theoretical world of the field are not necessarily the best practitioners. Although the gap between theory and practice is not unique to the field of student affairs, it may be more prevalent in the profession because theory was born after practice.

"Theory is unimportant because it is too diffuse."

Given the massive proliferation of theories regarding college students' development over the last two decades, "sift[ing] the good out from the goofy" (Upcraft, 1993, p. 265) has become increasingly difficult. National uniform characteristics of diversity—gender, race, intelligence, sexual orientation, disability, and age—create a matrix of theories that can be overwhelming. These subcategories of personhood may generate a sense of the relative uselessness of theory among student affairs staff in that they preclude generalizing among students. For example, Gilligan (1982) challenged Kohlberg's (1969) moral-development theory because of its incongruence with female students' moral-development paths (Kohlberg's research was performed exclusively with males). This deconstruction of student development theories (though in Gilligan's case clearly warranted) according to a growing list of subcategories may leave the impression among student affairs professionals that theories increasing diffuseness renders it comparatively impotent to guide their efforts in understanding students and constructing educational programs that are responsive to their developmental realities.

"Theory is unimportant because it conflicts with personal beliefs."

Some Christian student affairs professionals wholly disregard theory because they see it as rooted in secular humanism and the positivist ideal of science as the doorway to objective truth. Because student development theory in particular and much of theorizing in general begins with the wrong assumptions, it is unreliable for shaping their efforts in helping students develop. From this perspective, specific biblical injunctions regarding maturity and discipleship are sufficient sources for shaping understanding of and models for developing college students.

Our interest in offering the comments above is not to provide undue credence to a view that theory is unimportant. We simply wish to identify several contexts that offer realistic explanations as to why some student affairs professionals cannot give theory adequate attention. We would be less than honest to suggest that we do not struggle with these issues as well. In the midst of these potentially distracting voices, however, from a Christian perspective we wish to affirm the importance of theorizing in the field, and we do so for several reasons.

First, engaging theory is a natural byproduct of fulfilling a vocation in the student affairs profession. Not only is theorizing an integral part of the human condition but also the particular calling of student affairs practitioners necessitates an involvement with relevant theory; it not only comes with being human, it comes as part of doing the job. Moreover, as student affairs staff explore and uncover the truth and error of various theories, they augment their understand of college students' development and may become more adept in effecting desired outcomes through the programs and interventions offered. The sheer volume of research on college students' development, as indicated by a perusal of Pascarella and Terenzini's (1991) anthology, leaves a clear impression that at least some of the theorizing already completed must be useful. Ultimately, student affairs professionals' investment in theory ostensibly offers greater wisdom in accomplishing their work.

Second, we affirm the importance of theory because our own experience as well as the experiences of the students with whom we work indicate that the theories ring true if only in part, with some, or at certain times. For example, Perry's (1968) dualistic stage describes a particular student in a campus residence hall quite nicely; or, a conversation with a sophomore student indicates that they have made substantial progress in what Chickering (Chickering & Associates, 1981; Chickering & Reisser1993) refers to as "developing autonomy;" or, we discover in a student's journal for a Freshman Year Experience (FYE) course that she recently has had what Parks (1986) refers to as a "shipwreck" experience; or, in an orientation seminar we surmise that an entering African American student may be in an "immersion stage," based on W. Cross' (1978) typology; or, finally, in an exit interview with a graduating senior, we conclude that he is what Marcia (1980) calls "identity-foreclosed" and wonder what we might have done differently to help him develop differently. The point is simply this: theories assist student affairs practitioners in describing students and their experiences. As such, they offer a useful interpretive tool that may provide cues regarding how to help students learn.

Third, at the expense of sounding forlorn or oppressed, being versed in theory contributes positively to student affairs professionals' credibility with other colleagues. Because the student affairs field has incorporated its theory base from the social sciences and education, practitioners' familiarity with and competent articulation of these theories creates significant opportunities for dialog, collaboration, and partnership with many institutional partners. In addition, for those student affairs professionals who may feel like second-class citizens due to overt devaluing from colleagues, their own insecurities, or both, we suggest asserting interest in and becoming more discussant about the substantial body of theoretical research and knowledge that has been produced over the years. To be clear, student affairs professionals should not embrace theoretical reflection as a means of proving themselves to their detractors but as a professional obligation to fulfill the distinctive challenge of being excellent educators.

Finally, and particularly for those who profess Christian faith, we suggest that theory is important because it constitutes an arena in which a responsibility to shed light is necessary. We believe that Christian student affairs professionals must be fully versed in the theoretical wisdom of the profession in order to participate coherently and credibly in the ongoing dialogs and debates. God's call to those who may follow to be truth bearers is certainly applicable to the issue of theorizing. As a result, Christian student affairs practitioners must strive to keep theoretically astute by reading the relevant books and journals; listening with a discerning ear to extramural and intramural conversations and papers; and responding with informed, well-fashioned critique; burying heads in sand dunes clearly will not do, whether it may take the form of ignoring theory altogether or flippantly dismissing it without thoughtful reflection and analysis. The widespread theorizing that occurs within the student affairs profession implores Christians in the field not only to embrace the importance of theory but also to formulate and articulate responses that accurately reflect their worldview commitments. Later in this chapter, we offer a conversation among study group members that exemplifies this interest.

While not an exhaustive analysis of the importance of theory, the comments above underscore our commitment as Christians to the importance of theory in the student affairs profession. We do not, however, wish to create the impression of wholesale endorsement of all theories related to college students' development. Rather, from our perspective, the importance of theory must be balanced with the commitment to approach theory not only with a critical eye based on our worldview but also with an interest in linking theory to professional practice. It is to this discussion that we now turn.

Approaching Theory with Wisdom

In an earlier chapter, we presented wisdom as the ultimate goal of student learning. Perhaps it is fair to add that student affairs professionals do well to cultivate wisdom in their work, including how they approach theory. More specifically, we believe that student affairs practitioners must always treat theories with a critical eye and with a view toward how theory might shape student learning initiatives. We discuss each of these topics more thoroughly below.

Be Critical

Theorizing is never undertaken objectively. As we have stated elsewhere in this book, individuals, by nature, are guided by certain underlying assumptions about reality. As relates to an examination of student development theory, acknowledging that theories are not value-free is an important first step. Christians and non-Christians alike must be savvy at pinpointing the fundamental premises of theories and then assess the ways in which one's own worldview may complement, accommodate, or eschew.

Be Open

We reiterate for Christian readers that there is much to learn and use from theorists who may not share a biblical worldview. Based on what many theologians refer to as common grace, those committed to perspectives other than Christian ones are capable—at times even adept—at uncovering truthfulness, including truths about how college students develop. Although these theorists may approach their life and work with beliefs that are inconsistent with God's revelation, biblical wisdom dictates that, because they retain God's image, they may reveal aspects of life in ways that reflect God's intentions.

Be Humble

We initially included this subheading as a particular caution to Christian student affairs professionals who may be overly certain of all that is right and good. At a second glance, however, the admonition is easily applicable to other student affairs practitioners who "have it all figured out" based on some other point of view (e.g., humanist, feminist, critical theorist, pragmatist). To illustrate the nature of our concern here, we will use Christians as our example.

Christians, simply by virtue of being Christians, are not automatic purveyors of truth on all—or any—subjects. Rather, based on explanations offered in previous places in this book, Christians are prone to misrepresent, mistake, or simply miss God's desires for all areas of life. Though those committed to a Christian worldview appropriately take heart in God's restorative work and the directive and corrective orientation of the scriptural witness, they also acknowledge the persistent effects of an already-but-not-yet perfected life and world. As relates to student development theory, quick judgments based on knowledge of a theorist or an analysis of theory—"She's a behavioralist, so don't read any further," as well as, "He's a Christian, so his critique is right on"—are preemptive and wrong headed. In contrast to such a mindless approach, we believe that student development theories and their analyses, regardless of the worldviews of the people who produced them, are swirling blends of what a scriptural account refers to as "wheat and tares" (i.e., both good elements and bad elements based on one's point of view). The appropriate and challenging task, therefore, is to evaluate, sort, and sift carefully and graciously theoretical knowledge based on one's view of reality.

Discern Collaboratively

How does one begin to undertake the task of evaluating, sorting, and sifting theoretical knowledge? Or, to reiterate Upcraft's (1993, p. 265) phrase, "How do you sift the good out from the goofy?" Before we offer several questions that may help frame a critical approach to student development theory, we note that engaging in the work of theorizing and theory analysis in the context of community is eminently important. That is, assessing and applying theories that may lead to the acceptance, rejection, or adaptation of them, in part or in whole, is enhanced to the degree that it is undertaken communally (Van Leeuwen, 1985). For Christian student affairs professionals, this suggests that asking and answering questions about the wheat and tares of student development theory based on a Christian view is best accomplished in collaboration with others who share similar [Christian] convictions.

Though brief, the following questions provide an important grid from which Christian and non-Christian student affairs professionals alike may critique student development theory. More specifically, they may offer a useful starting point for Christian student affairs practitioners who may have heretofore either too quickly embraced a theoretical perspective as their own, or too quickly dismissed its potential contributions. To be clear, our particular interest here is threefold: to acknowledge that theory is important to our work, to proclaim that no theory is off-limits to Christian student affairs professionals, and to challenge Christians in the field to be keenly discerning as they approach the theoretical moorings of the field. The framing questions are:

* What are the theorist's assumptions?
* How was the theory generated?
* Does the theory evidence internal consistency?
* What is the theorist's view of humans?
* What does the theorist consider as good?

* What does the theorist consider as the goal?
* Does the theory find expression within your own experience?
* Does the theory tend to reduce persons to a singular aspect of their existence?
* Does the theory connect with other dimensions of life?
* Does the theory account for differences among persons?
* What aspects of the theory resonate/conflict with a Christian view of life?

Applying Theory To Practice

As we said earlier in this chapter, some student affairs practitioners—both Christian and non-Christian—discount the importance of theory. For them, applying theory to professional practice is a meaningless concept for the obvious reason that they lack the interest in—must less knowledge about—theory. For others within the field, however, who tacitly support the importance of theory, the gap between understanding the theory and using the theory to interpret and inform their jobs remains wide. Bloland, Stamatakos, and Rogers (1994, p. 11) are particularly clear on this point:

> despite the continual advocacy of student development theory as essential for program planning, very little of a practical, nuts-and-bolts nature, is presented for translating theory into campus programs . . . . In fact, theory may well have complicated and mystified the process of programming without materially improving it.

Whether the gulf between theory and practice in the student affairs profession occurs due to discarding theory at the outset or to neglecting important, ongoing translations; in either case, we lament the result—the nonapplication of theory to professionals' day-to-day work. Accordingly, Upcraft and Barr's (1990, p. 299) recommendations to "expand the theory base of our profession" and "get better at translating theory into practice" could not be more appropriate. Moreover, since many student affairs professionals characterize themselves as "experts on students," it is realistic to expect that they possess "a knowledge of student development theory and the ability to translate that theory into useful information to aid in planning, policy formation, and program development" (Barr & Albright, 1990, p. 193). Creamer (1980; 1990), in particular, has much to say in this regard, especially with respect to identifying the knowledge, skills, and issues pertinent to the application of "developmental status data [in]to programmatic interventions" (Creamer, 1990, p. 5) that reflect the interests of a particular educational community.

From our perspective, Christian student affairs professionals have an opportunity to make a significant contribution at precisely this point. Because a Christian worldview eschews fragmentation in favor of integration and connectedness, Christians view the theory-practice topic as a false dichotomy. That is, a biblical perspective views the application of theory as a normative consequence of developing the theory. In the same way that we previously made a case for the inextricable linkage between knowing and doing, theory building and theory implementing are two sides of the same coin given a Christian worldview. A biblical view underscores the inadequacy of *finding* a truth (i.e., or a theory) without its complementary partner, *living* a truth; Christians' interest in truth necessarily includes a commitment to embody truth. Given the innate sensibility of what may be referred to as the theory-with-practice approach within a biblical view of life, Christian student affairs professionals potentially have much to offer in improving this important aspect of student affairs. To do so effectively, however, will require Christian student affairs professionals to be engaged substantially more than they currently are in developing theoretical knowledge, in understanding the importance of theory, in thoughtfully critiquing theory supporting the field, and in defining their work in ways that provide adequate time to link theory with practice. The discussion among study group members which follows, is an attempt, at least in part, to heed this challenge.

A Discussion of Chickering's Theoretical Model

In February 1995, the study group assembled in a student conference room at Messiah College to put into practice what we have advocated in this chapter. Believing that analysis and critique is best done in community, we explored together a theory of college students' development. We selected Chickering's (1969; Chickering & Reisser, 1993) theory due to its relative popularity among student affairs professionals and also because of its historical dominance in the field. Needless to say, many readily recognize Chickering as the name associated with the seven vectors of human development, particularly as they find expression among college populations.

In advance of the conversation, we pondered the perspectival advice of several Christian authors who take seriously the matter of theory analysis and critique from a Christian point of view. For example, Van Leeuwen (1985) reminds us of the two skewed tendencies within the various theoretical systems of psychology, both of which have to do with particular views of the person. At one extreme, human beings may be viewed as the mere product of natural causes, or, on the other, as "the autonomous, self-correcting crown of evolution" (Van Leeuwen, 1985, p. xi). The dilemma is that both views represent a particular "moment of truth," in that each describes one aspect of our humanity. As Van Leeuwen (1985, p. xi) puts it: "we as persons are indeed related both downward to the material creation as well as upward to a transcendent creator . . . but the first [reductionistic] view takes too little account of the image of God in persons, while the second [triumphalistic] view takes too little account of human finitude and sin." Given that much of developmental theory borrows liberally from the field of psychology, we judged that Van Leeuwen's warnings about extremes may be relevant to our analysis of Chickering.

We also acknowledged a commitment to the scriptural witness as an authoritative guide for thought and life. Wolterstorff's (1988) comments regarding the exploration of patterns of shalom for human existence were particularly insightful. As such, we attempted to construct the analysis with delight, which, as Wolterstorff suggests, comes from shaping the pieces and patterns of one's life according to the divine blueprint of wholeness, harmony, and well-being.

Finally, we constructed several questions that would help to frame our discussion of the assumptions and resulting conclusions of Chickering's vector theory, as follows: What does Chickering consider to be good and to be goal? Where does Chickering's theory resonate with a Christian view and where is it dissonant? What is the relationship between Chickering's theory and student learning, particularly with respect to the principles and goal of student learning that we discussed earlier?

Before reading a transcript of our conversation, three provisos are in order. First, our discussion appears essentially in its original progression, though edited substantially for length. That is, it has not been significantly rearranged to achieve a more logical flow of ideas. Rather, it presents itself for what it is; that is, as a critical conversation among eight Christian practitioners. As such, its pattern is more spiral (i.e., both circular and progressing) than linear (i.e., straight line, point to point). Several different approaches to the issues are taken and the participants take the dialog back to key ideas for further elaboration and clarification.

Second, our conversation is not exhaustive. We engaged in what we consider an important activity for Christian [and all] student affairs professionals. As we stated at the outset of the book, however, the dialog is just beginning, especially among Christians. Discussing theories through eyes of faith is an ongoing challenge; carefully exploring the potential truths and untruths of these theories is a component part of the calling to be both Christian and student affairs professional. So, continue the conversation where we stopped. Amplify it with your own insights and observations shaped by your understanding of God's ways in the world. Extend it where we did not go; deepen it where we were shallow; correct it where we were in error. Whatever the case, do not avoid the conversation, and enter it seeking wisdom of God's world with particular emphasis on understanding college students' development.

Finally, it may be helpful to understand that Chickering views the purpose of higher education as human development. Although we do not share that perspective as such, we acknowledge that we may glean good things from his vector theory, especially as it may help educators understand college students. We include a particular excerpt from Chickering below since it was the focal point of much of our conversation:

> Like many humanistic models, this one is founded on an optimistic view of human development, assuming that a nurturing, challenging college environment will help students grow in stature and substance. Erikson believed in an epigenetic principle. Rogers saw a benign pattern at work in human beings, similar to the process that turns acorns into oak trees. The ancient Greeks had a concept alien to our modern-day emphasis on specialization and fragmentation between body and mind, between the physical and the spiritual. It is called *aretê*. According to the Greek scholar H. D. F. Kitto (1963, pp. 171-72), it was their ideal:
>
>> When we meet it in Plato we translate it "Virtue" and consequently miss all the flavour of it. "Virtue," at least in modern English, is almost entirely a moral word; *aretê* on the other hand is used indifferently in all the categories and means simply "excellence." It may be limited of course by its context; the *aretê* of a race-horse is speed of a cart + horse strength. If it is used, in a general context, of a man, it will connote excellence in the ways in which a man can be excellent - morally, intellectually, physically, practically. Thus the hero of the *Odyssey* is a great fighter, a wily schemer, a ready speaker, a man of stout heart and broad wisdom who knows that he must endure without too much complaining what the gods send; and he can both build and sail a boat, drive a furrow as straight as anyone, beat a young braggart at throwing the discus, challenge the Phraecian youth at boxing, wrestling, or running; flay, skin, cut up, and cook an ox, and be moved to tears by a song. He is in fact an excellent all-rounder; he has surpassing *aretê*.
>
> Kitto says that "this instinct for seeing things whole is the source of the essential sanity in Greek life" (p. 176). Institutions that emphasize intellectual development to the exclusion of other strengths and skills reinforce society's tendency to see some aspects of its citizens and not others. Just as individuals are not just consumers, competitors, and taxpayers, so students are not just degree seekers and test takers. To develop all the gifts of human potential, we need to be able to see them whole and to believe in their essential worth. In revising the seven vectors, we hope to offer useful tools to a new generation of practitioners who want to help students become "excellent all-rounders." We also hope to inspire experienced faculty, administrators, and student services and support staff to recommit to the mission of nurturing mind, body, heart, and spirit (Chickering & Reisser, 1993, pp. 40-41).

> *Jinny:*   In my mind, Chickering is pretty-up front about his assumptions. His comments on page forty seem to answer the

question, Who am I? He might say that humans are ultimately nice masters of the universe; people are the center of it all, they are in charge. But, I use the word *nice* to indicate that Chickering also refers to what might be regarded as a golden rule approach. When he talks about humanizing values, as balancing self-interests with those of others, it sounds like he holds for human beings' not being totally self-centered.

Jay: This seems like one place that we may have a fundamentally different view of reality than he does, particularly if you take the Fall seriously. It seems like he discounts the need for any salvation-redemption experience. For him, "man as the measure" serves as the crucial underpinnings for his model. If the foundation is wrong, then what he builds on top of it also will be wrong, at least in part.

Miriam: Would we agree with the second part of his sentence on page forty:"assuming that a nurturing, challenging college environment will help students grow in stature and substance?"

Barry: Do you think that's how he defines the human problem—as a lack of education or a lack of people to help others develop as humans? Is his remedy, then, to provide an intentionally orchestrated environment that helps people grow?

Jay: I think that I would argue that education alone, or the nurturing, challenging environment alone, is not sufficient to promote the type of change that we envision. One of the most highly educated cultures in history was Nazi Germany. It didn't prevent Auschwitz from happening. In more contemporary terms, we know that most college students could get an "A" on a test about factors that contribute to the spread of HIV, but knowing the facts doesn't necessarily result in appropriate behavior. Knowing the right stuff isn't sufficient.Even creating an environment in which sex education and condom machines in the residence halls are provided won't ensure that every college student will have sex with adequate—or anticipated—protection. There must be something more than the type of approach that Chickering and others humanistic thinkers propose.

Jinny: Two things occur to me. First, he doesn't address or recognize the problem of evil in the world. The most he says is that people may be flawed in a particular aspect of life. But, he also says that the resources to correct a flaw are within each human being. As Christians, we would take exception to that view. Second, I agree with Jay that Chickering doesn't seem to recognize the gap between what people may know and how they may behave. His concept of congruence is an attempt to address this gap but, once again, congruence is achieved by autonomous, individual effort over time.

Terry: To be fair, though, we would affirm that establishing a connection between belief and behavior is a process, both in our own lives as well as in the lives of the students with whom we work. It certainly doesn't happen overnight.

Bill: I have a question about his concept of excellent all-rounders. Does his all-rounder concept have any resemblance to a Christian view of an integrated person? To give him the benefit of the doubt, he acknowledges the limitations of fragmentation and desires something akin to wholeness. By amalgamating various development theories to create a kind of metatheory, however, I wonder if he actually achieves an integrated approach or just a whole- equals-the-sum-of-its-parts approach.

Kate: Bill, your comment reminds me that we must be careful not to read too much into his assumptions. He observed college students and wrote about what he saw. I don't mean to suggest that his work is value-free, it's just that responding to what he's written is a limitation. But, he's definitely making observations through some framework.

Dave: Pages forty and forty-one seem to be key in that regard. Like Bill said, Chickering does acknowledge a tendency toward reductionism and offers that it's inappropriate to reduce life to a particular aspect of life. We want to affirm this larger picture too, which he refers to as all-rounder. But, I wonder if a difference between Chickering and us is that we attach different meanings to some common words or phrases. For example, he mentions an *optimistic view, human development, nurturing, challenging college environments*, and *excellent all-rounders*. It's not as though we are against these things, it's just that we may have different interpretations of how these ideas might find expression.

Terry: I agree. His general emphasis seems to be on process rather than content. He uses all kinds of words and phrases—*emotions, responsible actions, inner direction, acceptance, stability, goals, commitment, values, authenticity,* and so on. All of these terms require content. Simply saying that it's all a process and that students have to move to higher stages in the process in each of these areas is insufficient. To omit a directional component to the structure seems to me to one of the greatest shortcomings of Chickering.

Dave: The other thing that surprised me was how easily what he says on pages forty and forty-one may apply outside of the college context. If you take out the word *college* in different places, is it still clear that we are talking about what happens in college? I mean *excellent all-rounder* could apply to what goes on in a church or a camp or in your home. One doesn't have to be in college to be part of a helping, nurturing environment. What relationship does his view have to the specific college context of student learning?

Jinny: I think Chickering would say that his vectors are a map for adult maturation that continues over a lifetime and that college is a very critical phase in this process. I think he would say that the vectors represent a journey that all human beings need to take, whether they go to college or not. It's just that college has a unique opportunity to be a catalyst for one's maturation. Maybe he would go so far as to say that college is a hothouse for vector movement as a person journeys to becoming a mature adult.

Bill: I think Chickering implies that if students don't develop in college, then the college has failed.

Kate: I agree. There's a sense in which his theory is an indictment of higher education for, at times, being too narrowly focused on the acquisition of knowledge and skills to the disregard of human development altogether.

Dave: But what might faculty members say about this issue? Wouldn't some of them say that human development is why student affairs staff are important?

Kate: I think that it may depend on the institution. If you asked faculty members if the purpose of college was for students to learn competence, develop integrity, and so on, I think many of them may agree.

Dave: But I wonder if they would say that it was their role to help students develop competence and emotional maturity, move from autonomy to interdependence, and so on.

Miriam: Although some faculty members may not say it quite the way Chickering discusses it, Burwell's research suggests that according to students, changes that take place in college occur through the classroom. Of course, other research suggests that plenty of students' development occurs outside the classroom as well.

Kate: One of the things that always intrigues me about Chickering is that he simply describes how students develop in college while not being real specific about what the change is attributable to. Since Chickering's appeal is largely to student affairs folks, we easily conclude that the development occurs outside the classroom, and we may too easily overlook the development that is effected through the classroom.

Barry: That makes me wonder if the development language that Chickering uses is conducive to the overall student learning context of college. Of course, maybe student affairs professionals make it worse by relegating it to their work alone rather than to the larger institutional context.

Bill: That raises the basic question: Do you think Chickering is useful? My sense is that many people think he is useful, including Christians that are in the student affairs field. I don't hear us saying, at least so far, that we should completely write him off.

Jay: I've always liked Chickering and his model for a number of reasons. As Kate suggested earlier, his beginning point was to observe what was happening to students in college and then describe it in a way that made sense. Such an approach has value. I also like it because, while it is a developmental model, it is not a lockstep model. It is a messy process; things are happening in different areas at the same time and it is not neatly sequential. There is a pattern, to be sure, and some experiences seem to precede other experiences. He also described a multidimensional process that doesn't as easily fall to the criticism of reductionism like other models that focus on one particular aspect of humanity. From my perspective, he provides some very helpful information about the group of people with whom we work. Common grace says that he has some good stuff here that we can take, build on, use—critique certainly—but apply quite usefully.

Terry: What other things are people saying that is useful about Chickering's vector theory. I think the reason why we picked him was because he is one of the better-known theorists.

Jay: At Messiah, I think we have an extra affinity for Chickering because we were part of his original sample for the small-college study. It's hard to fathom in the late 1960s that we would have been chosen as we were. But, it's interesting that there were at least some Christian students in his population who were in the original study.

Kate: I had forgotten that this study was sponsored by the Council for the Advancement of Small Colleges. When we go back to our comments about the image of wholeness that he developed, I wonder if this was part of what drove such an agenda. Small colleges were perhaps trying to argue that they were good because they developed the whole person, much more so than universities. Maybe Chickering's model was used, in effect, as a marketing tool for small colleges.

Terry: When you go to the second half of the book (establishing identity, developing purpose, developing integrity), these are the things that really do play well to the types of institutions in which we work.

Barry: Think about what might have been influencing him in the original study, things such as the Civil Rights movement and interest in individual freedom. Seen in that light, his interest in challenging colleges to be responsive to where students are and the issues that they face should come as little surprise. He's very much into a humanistic, person-centered perspective that was spawned in the sixties.

Dave: That may provide some clue as to why he modified one vector from the time of the first edition to the second. In the 1969 edition, he labeled the third vector "individual autonomy." Autonomy tended to be more of an issue in the late 1960s and early 1970s. In the 1993 edition, he labels this third vector, "moving through autonomy towards interdependence" which tends to resonate more with the ethos of the late 1980s and 1990s.

Kate: What has always been most useful to me is that he acknowledges an interplay between emotions and developmental tasks. Very few other developmental theories talk about the impact of emotions on that particular piece of development and vice versa or how they weave together. That has been the most useful to me.

Bill: I'm interested in getting back to pages forty and forty-one, where Chickering goes to great lengths to get at this word *aretê*, which he describes as a virtue of excellence in all aspects of life. Ultimately, we don't want to throw the Chickering "theory baby" out with the "application bath water," but we do want to press toward making sense of him from a Christian perspective, particularly with respect to his views about what takes place during college.

Jay: I think that *aretê* is used once or twice in the New Testament. The idea behind it is that something does what it is designed to do.

Regarding human beings, the idea is one of Christian maturity or perfection, of being and doing what one was created to be and do. The closer one gets to that, the more excellent he or she is.

Jinny: That's intriguing. So, what Chickering is doing is trying to figure out a design or purpose without knowing, acknowledging, or listening to a Designer.

Kate: Or having any sense that a larger design even exists.

Terry: I think that virtue, in its own right, is the design for Chickering. It doesn't have to be connected to a Designer per se. In other words, there's no purpose behind virtue or the pursuit of virtue per se; it just is. It simply serves as a standard to shoot for, about which there is no transcendent context or purpose. But, insofar as it exists for Chickering in that way, I guess that you could say that it has some meaning for him.

Dave: In that sense, this idea of virtue functions as one of Chickering's beliefs about life. And, it's connected to his notion of excellent all-rounders. In this context, his vectors' model makes sense; they are consistent with trying to develop humanness, which in the final analysis, may be the point for Chickering. I think that Christians have something much different to say both about the goal of development and the process of development.

Miriam: I wonder if we could shift to the vectors and try to ask some questions about them. He gives a description of the vectors as "major highways for journeying toward individuation, [which is] the discovery and refinement of one's unique way of being . . . and also toward communion with other individuals and groups." Even though people may use these highways differently, everyone has to traverse this map along the various vectors. So, what do we think about this?

Jay: I would like to make some remarks about the different vectors, too, particularly regarding how we might view them from a Christian perspective. Regarding Chickering's developing competence vector, his humanistic view seems to come through. As such, it seems to overlook the idea of giftedness or God's creative work in our lives.

Terry: I think that is related to what we said earlier about descriptive models. When you generalize, you can make something true about everybody and nobody at the same time. Descriptive models generally fail to account for the uniqueness in people. In a Christian context, uniqueness is often framed within the context of giftedness, in which the issue of being more unique or more the same as someone else is not the point.

Jinny: Regardless of the nature of generalizations, we certainly talk about competencies in higher education. For example, Chickering talks about intellectual competence as skill when using one's mind. He does not mention the responsibility that comes with knowledge, which would be much more clearly in view within a Christian worldview.

Bill: That's an important point that we've already touched on—knowledge to what end?

Kate: I think his approach is reflective of most humanists. Anything that comes out of a purely scientific framework divorces knowing from the responsibility of knowing. From my perspective, Christian higher education has bought into that division almost as much as have other institutions of higher ed. I think that even within Christian higher ed we often don't teach students the nature of the responsibility that accompanies knowing.

Terry: His understanding of competencies, though, may simply be linked to the idea that developing competence is part of development writ large and, as such, is a good thing. For example, I can't help but think that Chickering has been influenced by John Dewey. Dewey said that education does three things: it assimilates you into a larger culture, it provides more opportunity for an egalitarian experience, and it provides a certain civic virtue. When you look at Chickering's model, it seems easy to equate education and development, at least the way he lays it out.

Jinny: We have to bring this to a close so that we have sufficient time to address another topic. Thank you very much for your participation.

References

Astin, A. (1985). *Achieving educational excellence: A critical assessment of priorities and practice in higher education.* San Francisco: Jossey-Bass.

Barr, M., & Albright, R. (1990). Rethinking the organizational role of student affairs. In M. Barr, M. L. Upcraft, and Associates, *New futures for student affairs* (pp. 181-200). San Francisco: Jossey-Bass.

Bloland, P., Stamatakos, L., & Rogers, R. (1994). *Reform in student affairs: A critique of student development.* Greensboro, NC: ERIC Counseling and Student Services Clearinghouse.

Cass, V. (1979). Homosexual identity formation: A theoretical model, *Journal of Homosexuality, 4,* 219-35.

Chickering, A. (1969). *Education and identity.* San Francisco: Jossey-Bass.

Chickering, A., & Associates. (1981). *The modern American college: Responding to new realities of diverse students and a changing society.* San Francisco: Jossey-Bass.

Chickering, A., and Reisser, L. (1993). *Education and identity* (2nd ed.). San Francisco: Jossey-Bass.

Clouser, R. (1991). *The myth of religious neutrality: An essay on the hidden role of religious belief in theories.* Notre Dame, IN: University of Notre Dame Press.

Copland, B. (1989). Adult learners. In M. L. Upcraft and J. Gardner (Eds.), *The freshman year experience* (pp. 303-315). San Francisco: Jossey-Bass.

Creamer, D. (1980). *Student development in higher education: Theories, practices, and future directions.* Alexandria, VA: American College Personnel Association.

Creamer, D., & Associates (1990). *College student development: Theory and practice for the 1990s.* Alexandria, VA: American College Personnel Association.

Cross, K. (1981). *Adults as learners: Increasing participation and facilitating learning.* San Francisco: Jossey-Bass.

Cross, W. (1978). The Thomas and Cross models of psychological negrescence: A review, *Journal of Black Psychology, 5,* 13-31.

Erikson, E. (1950). *Childhood and society.* New York: Norton.

Feldman, K., & Newcomb, T. (1969). *The impact of college on students.* San Francisco: Jossey-Bass.

Fowler, J. (1981). *Stages of faith.* New York: Harper & Row.

Gilligan, C. (1982). *In a different voice: Psychological theory and women's development.* Cambridge: Harvard University Press.

Helms, J. (1984). Towards a theoretical explanation of the effects of race on counseling: A black and white model. *The Counseling Psychologist, 12* (4), 153-64.

Kohlberg, L. (1969). Stage and sequence: The cognitive-developmental approach to socialization. In D. A. Goslin (Ed.), *Handbook of socialization theory and research* (pp. 347-480). Chicago: Rand McNally.

Loevinger, J. (1976). *Ego development: Conceptions and theories.* San Francisco: Jossey-Bass.

Marcia, J. (1980). Identity in adolescence. In J. Adelson (Ed.), *Handbook of adolescent psychology* (pp. 159-87). New York: Wiley.

Miller, T., Winston, R., & Mendenhall, W. (Eds.). (1983). *Administration and leadership in student affairs.* Muncie, IN: Accelerated Development Inc.

National Association of Student Personnel Administrators (NASPA). (1989). *Points of view.* Washington, DC: NASPA.

Noel, L., Levitz, R., & Saluri, D. (Eds.) (1985). *Increasing student retention: Effective programs and practices reducing the dropout rate.* San Francisco: Jossey-Bass.

Parks, S. (1986). *The critical years.* San Francisco: Harper & Row.

Pascarella, E., & Terenzini, P. (1991). *How college affects students.* San Francisco: Jossey-Bass.

Perry, W. (1968). *Forms of intellectual and ethical development in the college.* Troy, MO: Holt, Rinehart, and Winston.

Piaget, J. (1964). *Judgment and reasoning in the child.* Patterson, NJ: Littlefield Adams.

Rogers, C. (1951). *Client-centered therapy: Its current practice, implications, and theory.* Boston: Houghton Mifflin.

Rogers, C. (1961). *On becoming a person.* Boston: Houghton Mifflin.

Sanford, N. (1967). *Where colleges fail.* San Francisco: Jossey-Bass.

Schlossberg, N., Lynch, A., & Chickering, A. (1989). *Improving higher education environments for adults.* San Francisco: Jossey-Bass.

Stroup, H. (1964). *Toward a philosophy of organized student activities.* Minneapolis: University of Minnesota Press.

Suppe, F. (1977). *The structure of scientific theories* (2d. ed.). Urbana: University of Illinois Press.

Tatum, B. (1992). Talking about race, learning about racism: The application of racial identity development theory in the classroom. *Harvard Educational Review, 62* (1).

Thomas, D. (1992). Church-related campus culture. In D. Guthrie and R. Noftzger, Jr. (Eds.), *Agendas for church-related colleges and universities* (New Directions for Higher Education, no. 79, pp. 55-63). San Francisco: Jossey-Bass.

Tinto, V. (1987). *Leaving college: Rethinking the causes and cures of student attrition.* Chicago: University of Chicago Press.

Upcraft, M. L. (Ed.). (1984). *Orienting students to college* (New Directions for Student Services, no. 25). San Francisco: Jossey-Bass.

Upcraft, M. L. (1993). Translating theory into practice. In M. Barr and Associates, *The handbook of student affairs administration* (pp. 260-73). San Francisco: Jossey-Bass.

Upcraft, M. L., & Barr, M. (1990). New futures for student affairs: A summary agenda. In M. Barr, M. L. Upcraft, and Associates, *New futures for student affairs* (pp. 295-301). San Francisco: Jossey-Bass.

Upcraft, M. L., & Moore, L. (1990). Evolving theoretical perspectives of student development. In M. Barr, M. L. Upcraft, and Associates, *New futures for student affairs* (pp. 41-68). San Francisco: Jossey-Bass.

Van Gennep, A. (1966). *The rites of passage.* Chicago: University of Chicago Press.

Van Leeuwen, M. (1985). *The person in psychology: A contemporary Christian appraisal.* Grand Rapids: Eerdmans.

Wolterstorff, N. (1988). *Reason within the bounds of religion* (2d ed.). Grand Rapids: Eerdmans.

Wright, D. (1984). Orienting minority students. In M. L. Upcraft (Ed.), *Orienting students to college* (New Directions for Student Services, no. 25, pp. 53-66). San Francisco: Jossey-Bass.

Chapter 6

Model Programs in Student Affairs

Jay H. Barnes and Kate Harrington

WE HAVE SPENT considerable time thus far speaking rather theoretically and abstractly about a Christian view of student affairs. One of the central questions on which the study group convened, however, concerned the practices of student affairs, namely: Do student affairs programs at Christian colleges operate any differently from those at other types of colleges? As we stated earlier, we wonder how often it has been the case that student affairs programs at Christian colleges uncritically borrow existing, fashionable paradigms, mix in some Christian principles, and apply the resulting paradigm to campus life. We are similarly concerned that the structures, titles, and programs of student affairs programs at Christian colleges frequently bear striking resemblances to those of other types of colleges and universities.

These similarities, at the very least, necessitate some reflection. Because we acknowledge that we begin with a particular [Christian] worldview, one might expect that we would produce unique institutional and student affairs structures, programs, approaches, and intended outcomes at least part of the time. Although it is certainly not the case that mainstream higher education and student affairs cultures have nothing good to offer, we wonder if Christian educational leaders have spent enough time considering how a Christian view is worked out in student learning in general and in student affairs in particular.

With these thoughts in mind, we thought that it would be useful to highlight several existing programs that appear to reflect a thoughtful Christian view. We identified these programs through two primary processes: (1) through informal professional networks, and (2) through a formal appeal to members of the Association for Christians in Student Development to submit descriptions of programs that exemplified Christian principles. Regarding the latter, we were intrigued that relatively few submissions were received. It may be that our colleagues were too busy to submit program descriptions. It may be, however, that even among ourselves we are unsure whether our programs are uniquely Christian.

As we discussed which programs to include, we were somewhat unclear as to how to define "exemplary" programs; we wished to avoid any sense of inappropriate competitiveness. We eventually concluded that the programs presented in this chapter should resonate, at least in part, with the principles of student learning outlined earlier. We settled on eight programs that generally represent a broad spectrum of typical student affairs functions. Some have formal names, some do not. After offering a brief description of each program, we highlight the components of student learning that it seems to reflect most clearly.

Before proceeding, several caveats are worth noting. First, our knowledge of these programs, for the most part, came from written descriptions from and brief phone conversations with, someone connected with the program. If we misrepresented or misunderstood a program, it was not intentional; more than likely, we simply lacked exhaustive information. Second, we do not offer these programs because we think that they are perfect, and we do not offer them because we believe that they should be duplicated on every campus. Rather, we offer them as illustrations of what might be done, as means of assisting Christian student affairs practitioners to assess their own programs, as ideas to spark conversations on individual campuses, and as examples of programs that evolved based on thoughtful reflection of the relationship between Christian beliefs and professional service. And, third, although we do not explicitly mention it in the remarks following each program, each program underscores student learning as its overarching context, and affirms itself as both a religious and purposeful endeavor.

Issachar's Loft at Messiah

Issachar's Loft is the name of the center for leadership and discipleship that began at Messiah College. Begun in 1992 under the direction of Doug Bradbury, the name is taken from a biblical reference in 1 Chronicles 12:32. Issachar was one of the twelve sons of Jacob, though almost nothing is known about him as an individual. In 1 Chronicles, however, reference is made to the people "of Issachar, who understood the times and knew what Israel should do." In examining a biblical view of what it means "to know," particularly regarding how people came to know God in Old Testament times, Bradbury concluded that gaining knowledge of God was a multidimensional activity involving heart, soul, mind, and strength; knowing was a complex and intimate activity. It is not coincidental that the Old Testament word for *know* is also a translation for the Old Testament word for sexual intercourse. A cognitive approach alone is obviously not sufficient!

According to Bradbury, other biblical principles emerged that were eventually applied to discipleship and leadership formation. Modeling, accountability, multidimensional approaches to gaining knowledge, exploring approaches that connect rather than categorize individuals, and activity and application balanced by silence and reflection became the basis for the new program. As the program developed, it took on several dimensions. For example, "Who's Zooming Who," a weekly Bible study, attracts approximately ninety students and is a point of entry into the program. This session, which provides students with general biblical knowledge as well as interpretation and application skills, is complemented by small-group opportunities under the leadership of a peer mentor. The smaller group provides not only a chance to reflectively apply what has been discussed in the large-group context, but it also reflects a modeling component of learning as well as provides leadership opportunities for peer mentors.

An emphasis on accountability is evident in several ways. Some students participate in a core group that focuses on accountability and leadership development. This core group helps to provide leadership for a variety of Loft functions. This is a place for honest discussion and peer confrontation about the application of biblical principles to daily living. A smaller accountability group also meets and is a place for a no-holds-barred approach to biblical discipleship.

Issachar's Loft demonstrates multidimensional approaches to learning through adventure activities such as caving, rock climbing, and initiative games. While the physical dimensions of these activities are challenging and invigorating, the components that precipitate significant learning are the group evaluation of the experience, individual reflection, and selected biblical teachings that relate to the experience. As such, the overall experience—the activity plus the debriefing—offers a unique way of learning. These principles and lessons are applied and extended in other ways for students who may take advantage of extended adventure activities, such as an annual trip to Haiti.

Using the expertise and facilities that Bradbury has developed, bridges have been built to other areas of campus as well. Bradbury works with many classes, sports teams, and campus organizations to help them develop a sense of unity and improved communication. Since unity, community, and communication are highly valued at Messiah, the services offered through Issachar's Loft simultaneously reflect the institution's mission, solidify biblical principles for relationships, and creatively contribute to student learning out of the classroom.

Within this program it is easy to identify the ways in which many of the principles of student learning are practiced. The emphasis on linking biblical principles to the issues and questions that Messiah students face demonstrates a wisdom-focused perspective. That is, Issachar's Loft provides an innovative framework in which students are challenged to remember, discern, and explore, as indicated in chapter 3. In addition, the program utilizes a multidimensional, yet integrated approach to help students link knowledge and experience that they have gained in particular activities with other aspects of their lives, both in and out of the classroom. Finally, Issachar's Loft clearly demonstrates a commitment to the communal aspect of learning; whether in large group or small group, whether entering the program or a mentoring within the program, whether on a ropes course or in a Bible study, the program emphasizes that learning is not an individualistic endeavor.

The CD Program at Calvin

The Cultural Discerner (CD) program at Calvin College is a component of its overall student activities program. Although Calvin has a long tradition of student activities based in residence life, athletics, the arts, and other areas of campus life, it did not have a formal student activities program until 1993. At that time Ken Heffner was hired as the Director of Student Activities and was charged with developing a student activities program that reflected a Christian worldview. Heffner began by asking some critical questions: What would a college student activities program have looked like in a pre-Fall world? How would Jesus have viewed student activities, leisure time, contemporary music, and popular media? Is there a reason for students to have to choose between Jesus and U-2? Needless to say, these questions typically are not asked when one is designing student activities programs. According to Heffner, they provided the appropriate context for creating a program that ultimately proclaims, "We have no need to fear the world." Rather than assist students in avoiding the world of popular culture, Calvin students are being challenged with ways of seeing music, comedy, television, and the like with Christian discernment.

The CD program exists to nurture Heffner's vision for student activities. CDS are Calvin students in each residence hall whom Ken trains to lead discussions with their peers about popular culture. The CDS parallel resident assistants (RAs) and other residence hall student leaders but have a different mission. Their role is to organize formal and informal programs that help students "learn to discern." For example, they facilitate a discussion in the residence hall about a recently released movie or about the lyrics of a particular musician. They help students come to terms with artifacts of popular culture from a Christian perspective by asking questions such as: Is this an excellently done film or song? Why or why not? What are the artists doing or saying that is right or wrong? On what basis do you make such an evaluations? How would you critique the message of a particular medium from an economic perspective, an aesthetic perspective, a gender perspective—all of which are informed by a Christian view?

Although these forums are not always easy, particularly because they occur within a Christian community that retains certain [negative] impressions of popular culture, Heffner is committed to sustain an activities program that rides on the edge. He admits that, at times, it is not clear which side of the edge one is on; the danger of running over people who are not yet ready to see or hear certain viewpoints clearly exists. According to Heffner, however, if one considers the popular arts as a place of spiritual battle, then no media is safe from the distortion of sin and no media is beyond Christ's redemption. As a result, the challenge looms large for reflective Christian students, and the process of learning about popular culture through a Christian lens is both exciting and boundless.

Perhaps one area that best demonstrates this challenge is in the area of music. Even to the casual observer, that music is particularly important to today's college students is eminently clear. Music helps to inform students' values and behaviors. From Heffner's perspective, if Christian students learn to be discerning regarding the gift of music, their lives are changed. Their decisions are no longer shaped primarily by so-called rules that automatically label certain music bad and other music good; nor are they influenced by an absence of rules altogether that render all music simply music—about which they have particular preferences to be sure. Rather, they are shaped by a radical commitment to implement Christ's redemptive power in experiencing and evaluating popular culture.

As Heffner looks for artists to bring to campus, he looks for Christians who are doing innovative work or non-Christians who have something important to say. He is quick to add that student activities programs are not to entertain or amuse students, although entertainment is appropriate in some settings. Rather, as part of a college that is committed to shaping the next generation, he considers these programs as learning opportunities that are signposts to a Christian view of life in general and the popular arts in particular. As such, the student activities program at Calvin is designed as a classroom on the popular arts in which students will both be exposed to new ideas as well as learn to discern wheat and tares from a Christian perspective.

Perhaps the two characteristics of learning most clearly embodied by Heffner's activities programming are its focus on wisdom development and integration. Helping Calvin students clarify their Christian beliefs (remembering), employ them as the grid through which to interpret popular culture (discernment), and encourage them to investigate this area further and more deeply (exploration) reflect the program's commitment to a wisdom-focused learning strategy. In addition, because Heffner develops much of his programming in collaboration with various academic departments—particularly music, art, communications, and English—it models for students the connectedness between more formal and less formal learning. Such collaboration has also yielded a communal approach to student learning as faculty members and students uncover analyses, critiques, and perspectives in both classroom and out-of-classroom settings.

When No One Is Looking at Mt. Vernon Nazarene

Michael Clyburn arrived at Mt. Vernon Nazarene College as the Dean of Student Development in 1992. He was welcomed by a student handbook that was approximately one hundred pages long, including twenty pages of prescriptive rules regulating student behavior. As is the case with many student handbooks, no one read it unless he or she was in trouble. Clyburn desired to reconstruct Mt. Vernon Nazarene's student handbook such that it would better account for the college's heritage, more thoughtfully reflect biblical guidelines for community life, and be read by students.

Clyburn began the redesign of the handbook in conjunction with the college's Campus Life Council. The document that they eventually produced was then forwarded to Mt. Vernon Nazarene's president, who added particular emphases as well. By the fall of 1993, the document was approved by the college's governing body and distributed to students. Entitled "Understanding the Lifestyle Guidelines of Mount Vernon Nazarene College," the new handbook focuses on the question, "What kind of person are you when no one is looking?" The document is based on various biblical assumptions that reflect the college's denominational heritage. For example, based on scriptural references such as Hebrews 12, 1 Corinthians 9, and Philippians 3, students are challenged to lay aside sin; develop the discipline, endurance, and winning spirit that reflect Christlike character; and pursue a "more pure, selfless lifestyle." Further, the document stresses the importance of moral choices and moral consequences, promoting the notion that the development of Christian character and values extends "far beyond a few years spent on campus."

From Clyburn's perspective, since the release of the new handbook, students have developed a significantly greater awareness and understanding of the college's expectations. Less confusion exists regarding fundamental issues, greater compliance with college policies has resulted, and students have a better sense of the institution's heritage and its continuing relationship to community responsibility. In addition, faculty members view the new handbook as a valuable tool in communicating Mt. Vernon Nazarene's history and expectations to students and other publics.

The document readily acknowledges that not all students will agree with the lifestyle guidelines contained in the document. At the very least, the guidelines will not be equally valued by Mt. Vernon Nazarene students. Acknowledging the reality of potential differences, a central feature of the document is a code of honesty that asks students to remove themselves from the college community if they are unwilling to *comply* [emphasis ours] with college expectations.

Although Mt. Vernon Nazarene's Lifestyle Guidelines is a not a program per se, we included it in this chapter to demonstrate how a wisdom-focused student learning perspective interpreted through the lens of an institution's religious heritage may even apply to the establishment of college policies. Whether one agrees with the particular content of the guidelines is secondary to the idea that the document was reflectively developed to promote an integrated learning community in which learning and behavior are inextricably related. Insofar as students pursue learning and lifestyle with a view toward developing Christlike character, they are growing in wisdom. We should also note the emphasis that this example places on community. Not only was the document communally created, the guidelines are ultimately intended for the entire community (faculty and students), and, as such, accountability is a communal issue as well.

Student Discipline at George Fox

If Mt. Vernon Nazarene serves as an example of policy development in the context of wisdom-focused student learning from a Christian perspective, George Fox College offers a model program regarding how to respond to students who may violate institutional policies. Based on scriptural references that describe characteristics of Christian believers (Colossians 3) and that outline a strategy for confrontation (Matthew 18), Deb Lacey devised George Fox's student discipline procedures. Formerly the Vice President for Student Life, Lacey had a special interest for students whom she referred to as "wounded dreamers." These students, found on every college campus, seem alienated from family, church, and faith, and struggle with institutional expectations and connections. In trying to think of better ways to reach these students, George Fox's process-oriented approach to student discipline emerged.

In applying Matthew 18 to breaches of college rules, the George Fox community stresses the need for peers to approach one another directly when an inappropriate action is observed. The person doing the confronting is expected to exhibit the personal qualities outlined in Colossians 3: compassion, kindness, humility, gentleness, patience, and forgiveness. If these attitudes are not present, the likelihood of a good confrontation will be difficult if not impossible. If the confronted person responds with repentance and changed behavior, no further action is necessary. If, however, the confronted student responds in an untoward manner, other professional staff become involved.

When confrontation is necessary beyond a peer, the process has three key ingredients: a team approach, fervent prayer, and follow-up. A typical team consists of two resident directors (RDs) and a student life associate dean. The team begins by praying together about the student and the situation. Because it is Lacey's conviction that professionalism without Christian maturity will not produce appropriate "fruit," team meetings should include prayer as a means of helping staff focus on relevant issues in their own lives as well as in the life of the student involved. After praying, the team meets with the student to hear his or her interpretation of the facts. Committed to be agents of God's grace in the situation, team members attempt to speak truthfully as well as seek the truth in the situation. After the meeting, the team reflects on the student's story, prays again, then makes a decision, and if the student is found negligent, determines appropriate sanctions.

Following the process, the student involved is connected with a member of the student life staff or a small group of student colleagues and staff members. In keeping with the tradition to which George Fox subscribes, Lacey believes that if a student has been loved through the process, if the truth has been spoken, and if the team has been sensitized through prayer to be agents of God's grace, then God will honor their efforts and ultimately good will eventuate.

Although discipline is seldom easy, George Fox has attempted to frame it within the context of their own Christian rendering of wisdom-focused student learning. Needless to say, the process and communal aspects are frontispieces in George Fox's program of student discipline. Even if a disciplinary situation never reaches an administrative level, students understand that out-of-class learning at George Fox is predicated on established expectations, mutual commitment to community, and interpersonal processes of growth and development. Moreover, such an approach to student discipline underscores an awareness of helping students grow in wisdom by calling constant attention to biblical moorings as the truth is sought, decisions are rendered, and further interaction and communication ensues.

Nutrition 1985 at Whitworth

To our knowledge, the following program does not currently exist on any college campus, although it did at one time. We believed that it was important to include, however, because it embodies many of the components of wisdom-focused student learning in Christian perspective and does so in an area that is commonly perceived as an ordinary service issue of the student affairs profession—food service.

Nutrition 1985, which occurred at Whitworth College in the same year, was offered as an alternative meal plan for students. The goal of the program was to educate students about issues of personal nutrition and world hunger and to generate awareness regarding the earth's dwindling resources. At the most basic level, Nutrition 1985 was an alternative meal plan that offered students the opportunity to eat healthily. In its fullness, however, the program provided an opportunity for students to understand economic, political, and ecological implications of their food choices.

Students who enrolled in the plan ate together in a separate dining room on campus. Menus reflected intentional strategies to eat less protein, more fresh and seasonal food rather than processed food, and to waste as little food as possible. Because food choice is often an issue with political overtones (as seen in the boycotting of grapes in order to draw attention to migrant workers), students understood that certain foods might be eliminated or used sparingly. The ecological implications of food choices included the energy required for cooking, storing, and transporting food; therefore, menus were planned with these issues in mind as well.

The program was managed by a steering committee and four subcommittees, each of which was comprised of dining service personnel, students, and faculty advisors. The steering committee focused on developing and ensuring the implementation of the goals of the program. The four subcommittees (Politics and Current Events; Energy, Ecology and Economics; Nutrition; and Christianity and Ethics) were responsible for educating students regarding specific issues and for implementing the goals of the steering committee in these respective areas. Seminars, presentations, films, service opportunities, and other activities were used as methods of educating the entire campus.

Nutrition 1985 clearly illustrates the capacity to infuse a common service function with learning objectives. It reflects an obvious interest in helping students grow in wisdom in that students were taught to discern a responsible approach to eating by applying biblical considerations of stewardship. Similarly, the program was integrated in that students relied on classroom knowledge and experiences to inform this approach and vice versa. Nutrition 1985 also evidenced multidimensionality by involving students at various levels of concern, including cognitive, affective, social, and moral dimensions of life. Finally, the program stressed the communal nature of learning by emphasizing interpersonal and group support structures while concomitantly taking practical action that corresponded to their religious, political, economic, and ecological concerns.

Service Learning at Waynesburg

A growing arena of activity within higher education and often within the purview of a student affairs office is service learning. The term *service learning* may connote many things to many people. For some, it represents little more than a new label for the volunteer, service-oriented programs that have existed for many years on many campuses. As meant here, however, service learning refers to the programmatic efforts to make service opportunities an alternative pedagogy within classroom courses. Faculty members are asked to consider how course content may be obtained or expanded using practical service experiences. Similarly, service opportunities provide a real-life context for students to test the theories, approaches, and perspectives garnered in classrooms. Through these experiences, students are expected not just to volunteer in a service area but to fulfill an intentional service opportunity, then to reflect and articulate what they learned through the experience viz-à-viz their simultaneous classroom education.

Service learning may ostensibly fit within any course in the formal curriculum. For example, at Azusa Pacific University, service learning is a required feature in course offerings in art, physical education, computer science, and Christian ministry. At Waynesburg College, however, educators have developed the Service Learning Course as a required component of its general education requirement. The course, which includes a minimum of thirty hours of service, involves various readings on current social events, the completion of a journal, regular meetings with a service mentor, a final paper that explores the proper role of government in community assistance, and an evaluation by the service placement supervisor.

We cannot speak highly enough of the added learning dimension that service learning offers to students' college experience, whether undertaken by Christian or non-Christian colleges alike. Learning principles of multidimensionality, integration, and process are clearly manifest in service learning programs. They not only create opportunities to learn in different venues (i.e., both cognitive and experiential based learning), but they also stress the necessary and reciprocal connection between what students learn both in and out of the formal classroom. In addition, service learning seems to offer a natural ebb and flow to the overall learning experience as students read books, hear lectures, and apply the formal classroom in a service capacity that is particularly relevant to the course—and vice versa. Finally, service learning is a de facto communal learning experience. Pressing students to move beyond the proverbial ivory tower of academe, service learning establishes links with community organizations and persons and may afford both faculty and students opportunities to learn together outside of the classroom.

Residence Life and Learning at Northwestern

No description of student affairs programs would be complete without including a program featuring residence life. For many campuses, including most Christian colleges, residence life is a major part of a student's experience. One wonders, however, whether the residence hall experience adequately fulfills its potential for helping students learn (Schroeder, Mable, & Associates, 1994).

One institution that is striving to maximize the opportunities for student learning in residence life is Northwestern University (IL). Although Northwestern is not a Christian college, we include an aspect of its residence life program because it captures many of the principles of wisdom-focused student learning that we believe reflect Christian principles. We reiterate that this is entirely possible and perhaps even likely. A college may embrace principles and purposes of student learning that resonate with a Christian view as such but may predicate such approaches on beliefs other than Christian.

Northwestern operates a program called residential colleges. Ranging in size from thirty-six to three hundred students and focusing on a variety of interests, Northwestern has eleven such residential colleges. Each college is headed by a faculty member who serves as the college "master." Faculty associates and a graduate student support the activities of the college. Other faculty members may volunteer to serve as faculty associates to the college. Students must apply for membership. Most residential colleges are structured around a theme that provides a focus for academic and social programming. Students work with their respective college masters to shape the programming within the college. For example, each college offers a program called "Firesides," which are informal presentations on a wide variety of subjects that are of interest to residents. In addition, residential college tutorials are given for academic credit to students who choose to enroll. These tutorials allow students and professors to explore mutual interests in far greater depth than is generally possible in standard classes.

Two obvious principles illustrated by Northwestern's residential colleges are integration and community. The program underscores the notion that learning is not expected to cease when students go back to the dorm. Rather, their living environment is an active continuation of the learning process; it may even be a more dynamic learning experience than students receive in formal classroom settings. Moreover, the nexus of faculty, staff, and student involvement creates a web of learning that is both communal and connected. Although the size, facilities, and resources of Christian colleges may detract from the ease with which they might implement such a program, we exhort Christian colleagues not only to consider residential colleges an important and excellent program but also one that resonates with a Christian view of student learning.

American Studies Program at the Coalition

The American Studies Program in Washington, DC, is the oldest and one of the most successful programs of the Coalition for Christian Colleges and Universities. Headquartered in a facility that is eight blocks from the Capitol, the program hosts approximately fourty students each semester from the ninety-plus member institutions of the Coalition. This creative program is intentionally interdisciplinary, examining public policy from sociological, political, theological, economical, and philosophical viewpoints.

According to Steve Garber, a faculty member in the program, the life of Christ offers the deepest truths about teaching. The structure and approach of the American Studies Program is a creative attempt to put Christ's model into practice in a way that changes the nature of the teaching/learning experience and challenges the status quo in American higher education. To properly appreciate what the American Studies Program is trying to do, it is instructive to probe this model more deeply.

According to Garber, Jesus was born into the world and was raised in a culture that was politically Roman but theologically Hebrew. Jesus' way of looking at the world was Hebraic, which meant that knowing and doing were inseparably linked; one did not know unless one did. Jesus, the Master-Teacher, worked out this linkage in three ways. First, people learned by seeing the truth done. Jesus always invited people to journey with him, to watch him live. His disciples may offer the quintessential example. Second, Jesus showed that people learn what is true by doing what is true. Thus, it comes as little surprise that Jesus sent his disciples out to test if and what they may have learned. And, third, Jesus emphasized the importance of seeing the truth demonstrated by those who indicated that they understood the truth. Stated another way, Jesus thought it necessary to practice what was preached. Perhaps this explains why his harshest words were reserved for hypocrites.

The American Studies Program strives to make these three principles relevant in their semester-long program by combining interdisciplinary seminars, internships, and group living. Through formal-and-informal classroom conversations with students, Coalition faculty help students understand that "ways of knowing are not morally neutral, but morally directive," (Schwehn, 1993, p. 94) that responding to a calling is more important than crafting a career, and that a Christ-centered worldview should result in a visibly Christ-centered way of life. As students come to the campus, usually with a concern for the larger world and a sense of willingness to leave the comforts of the familiar, they are challenged and supported to connect their Sunday-morning persona with their experiences during the remainder of the week—in the classroom, in their internship, and in their living environment. As such, the American Studies Program helps students wrestle with making sense of it all, with exploring whether their ultimate commitments as Christians are sufficient to provide understanding, direction, and vision to their personal and civic lives (Garber, 1994).

The American Studies Program may be an archetypal embodiment of Christ-centered, wisdom-focused student learning. Its emphasis on knowing and doing; its combination of living and learning in classroom, internship, and residence alike; its commitment to formal and informal faculty and student interaction; and, its emphasis on remembering, discerning, and exploring clearly resonate with our emphases in an earlier chapter. Although Christian colleges cannot replicate the size and opportunities of the American Studies Program, the challenge remains to fashion learning experiences that link knowing and doing in meaningful ways for students and in ways that correspond with particular institutional distinctives. Houghton College's and Messiah College's urban campuses in Buffalo and Philadelphia respectively, Azusa Pacific University's Mexi-Cali and Bridge projects, and Wheaton College's Summer Missions Projects are excellent examples of intentional efforts to link Christian faith with knowing, doing, and living. We encourage other Christian colleges to investigate similar opportunities. In the meantime, however, we also encourage Christian student affairs professionals (as well as Christian educators in general) not to overlook existing programs that, with some rethinking, reshaping, or expansion, might more fully reflect a Christian rendition of wisdom-focused student learning. Insofar as we do not retreat from such a challenge, we inch closer to our calling to consider and to enact our professional roles without ignoring our ultimate commitments.

For additional information on programs described in this chapter, contact:

Messiah College
Grantham, PA 17027

Ken Heffner
Director of Student Activities
Calvin College
3201 Burton St. S.E.
Grand Rapids, MI 49546

J. Michael Clyburn
Dean of Student Development
Mt. Vernon Nazarene College
800 Martinsberg Rd.
Mt. Vernon, OH 43050

George Fox College
414 North Meridian Street
Newberg, OR 97132

Rick Jones
Service Learning Coordinator
Waynesburg College
Waynesburg, PA 15370

Nancy Anderson
Northwestern University
Scott Hall, Room 8
601 University Place
Evanston, IL 60208

Steve Garber
American Studies Program
327 Eighth Street NE
Washington, DC 20002

References

Garber, S. (1994). *Learning to care: The transformation of higher education.* Unpublished manuscript.

Schroeder, C., Mable, P., & Associates. (1994). *Realizing the educational potential of residence halls.* San Francisco: Jossey-Bass.

Schwehn, M. (1993). *Exiles from Eden: Religion and the academic vocation in America.* New York: Oxford University Press.

Chapter 7

Reframing Student Affairs and Higher Learning

Kate Harrington

THE PREVIOUS CHAPTERS provide a nascent effort to utilize a Christian worldview in understanding higher education and, more particularly, the student affairs profession. A brief history of the profession in the larger context of the academe indicated the nature of its emergence and the underlying purposes, functions, and methods it embraced. Our conversations, wonderings, and struggles to articulate a purpose for student affairs that honored both the history of the field as well as our Christian perspective, however, prompted us to frame a new raison d'etre for the profession, namely wisdom-focused student learning. By offering this idea, we do not intend that the role of theory be discarded or diminished. In fact, the promotion of wisdom-focused student learning necessitates an understanding of theory and considerable care in using it to help students learn most effectively. Moreover, as we stated in the previous chapter, Christian student affairs practitioners must be discerning in this process whether developmental theories or more general learning theories are involved. This chapter is intended to explore the practical implications of the concepts presented in this book. It is designed to answer the question: Where do we go from here? More specifically, what might a thoughtful Christian student affairs professional do at this point?

Before outlining several suggestions, we wish to underscore that the very process of writing this book was a wisdom-focused learning experience for us. Perhaps the most useful suggestion that could come from our experience is that student affairs practitioners engage in a serious, ongoing conversation in the spirit of defining their work and its underlying purpose. Evaluating what one does and why as well as identifying new vistas for thinking and acting requires time and commitment. As a study group, we have explored these issues together for almost four years. The perspectives that we finally presented are not the ones we may have offered when we began. If we are to promote wisdom-focused learning with the students with whom we work, however, it seems reasonable to suggest that we model such learning ourselves.

An appropriate place to begin is by asking ourselves questions about our practice. We ordered the chapters of this book intentionally as a means of outlining how such an inquiry might proceed. Thus, the sections that follow, corresponding to the chapters that precede, serve as a study guide of sorts to critique practice and expose arenas in which revision or change may be useful. The questions in each section below may be used both for personal reflection and for structured dialog among divisional colleagues. Whatever the case, our intent is that the conversation not end with the reading of this book but extend into the offices, residences, classrooms, and coffee shops in which student learning takes shape.

Acknowledging a Worldview

As presented in the first chapter, all persons possess a worldview or a set of assumptions that provide meaning and direction to life. Saying that someone has a worldview is not the same thing as saying that someone is a Baptist or Catholic; membership in a denomination is not a prerequisite to having a worldview. Rather, everyone makes assumptions about the nature of persons, the purpose of society, the meaning of existence, and so on—and lives out these   assumptions as well. Not everyone, of course, holds the same assumptions. Further, individuals with similar assumptions may appropriate them quite differently. Some individuals may be quite unaware of their ultimate beliefs. Others may not perceive connections between beliefs and actions. Still others may not practice what they preach; theory in action conflicts with espoused theory. The point is simply this: Exploring the contours of our worldviews is an important first step in framing who we are, why we exist, and the relationship among these queries and our professional work.

On the surface, it may appear that Christians—compared to non-Christians—are automatically engaged with these theological- or philosophical-sounding   issues.   Our   experience,   however,   suggests   that   many persons—Christians and non-Christians alike—spend insufficient time examining their fundamental assumptions. As a result, we think it is helpful to begin by considering a set of questions:

*   What do I believe about people? Are they essentially good? bad? both? Can people change? How? What is their purpose? Is it attainable? Why or why not? Are differences among them good? bad? both? How do people function? What should people "do?" Why?
*   What is good? bad? Why is what is good good and what is bad bad? What is the greatest good? the worst bad? Where do good and bad

come from? Are things mostly good or bad? Will things always be that way? Why or why not? Why does life exist?

* How do I know? What is true? Does truth exist? Does truth matter? Is truth knowable? If so, how does one come to know it? What role does reason, feelings, experience play in relationship to truth?

How one responds to these questions is significant because responses to these questions shape how one makes sense of life; similarly, as one makes sense of life, he or she further fashions responses to these questions. How these questions are addressed has implications for the context, content, purpose, and people of higher education as well. How and why education takes place on every campus—Christian and non-Christian alike—reflects partial, evolving responses to these questions.

The process of examining and making explicit one's fundamental assumptions takes time and energy. At an institutional level, some exploration of written sources will be necessary to understand how a college—or a student affairs division—defines its underlying assumptions and the practices that take shape around them. In any case, we consider such a process a necessary place to begin in understanding who we are and what we do as educators, as well as why.

Exploring Historical Contexts

To understand where one is, it is useful to explore how one got there. Chapter 2 addressed this idea by outlining the historical development of the student affairs profession, highlighting important influences that shaped the philosophy and practice of the profession. In turn, we believe that it may be a helpful and illuminating exercise for student affairs departments to perform their own historical analyses. Perusing archives and official institutional histories and conducting personal interviews will help to create a historical context for understanding current realities of the student affairs division and the institution alike. We suggest focusing such an analysis around the following questions:

* For what purpose was the institution started? Is there a parallel between the history of the institution and the history of higher education in general?
* What is the stated mission of the institution currently? How has it evolved?
* For Christian colleges, what historical or present factors have influenced the theological identity of the institution, such as denominations, affiliations with parachurch organizations, and so on?
* When did student affairs first surface in the institution's history?

* Is there a parallel between the history of the student affairs division and the history of student affairs in general?
* What is the philosophy and purpose of the student affairs division? How has it evolved and why?
* How does the purpose/philosophy of the student affairs division relate to the purpose/philosophy of the institution?
* What were the points at which changes occurred within the division? What precipitated these changes?
* What forces are affecting the division at the present time? Can these forces be better understood in the context of the history?
* Have the tradition of the institution and the personalities of those present at any given time influenced which structures/purposes emerged?

Learning to take a historical view can enable one to better understand the present and plan for the future. Chief among the mistakes to be avoided are the establishment of activities or programs that run counter to the tradition of the school. Thinking historically can also help one gain and maintain perspective by recognizing that events within an institution often occur in cycles. And lastly, a historical perspective can often enable one to predict more accurately what might be effective in the future.

Emphasizing Wisdom-Focused Student Learning

The fundamental activity of higher education is student learning. Chapter 3 demonstrated that a Christian worldview affirms the primacy of learning as a human activity. This chapter differentiated between student learning and other emphases in undergraduate education and suggested that the focus of the student affairs profession should also be student learning. We further elaborated on student learning as a religious, purposeful, multidimensional, integrated, communal, processual, and wisdom-focused endeavor. It is likely that these principles of student learning, particularly if taken individually, transcend a Christian worldview and may be compatible with other worldviews as well. Nevertheless, the question to be asked at both individual and institutional levels is: What are the principles of learning suggested by the professed worldview? Asked another way: What is the relationship between ultimate beliefs and the educational enterprise? Further: To what degree do efforts in enacting student learning principles reflect one's deepest values about life?

Our own work is an effort to provide answers to these questions based on our Christian convictions. The centrality of student learning in the academy, the principles of student learning, and the purpose of student learning to develop wisdom are all conclusions that we earnestly believe reflect a Christian point of view. In addition, because we think that "Christian colleges are not automatically holy" (Guthrie, 1994, p. 228) by virtue of the fact that they identify themselves as Christian, we attempted to provide some further clues in Chapter 4 regarding how these principles and purposes may take shape in Christian institutions in general and, more specifically, among Christian student affairs practitioners at Christian colleges. With a particular interest in helping these institutions and Christian student affairs professionals further shape student learning in ways that best reflect their basic Christian beliefs, we developed the following series of evaluative questions:

* How would you describe your institution's purpose?
* What are the ultimate beliefs that underlie institutional purpose?
* What is the relationship, if any, between institutional purpose and the ultimate beliefs that lie at the foundation of the college?
* Is student learning an appropriate way to define the purpose of your institution? the purpose of the student affairs division?
* What does the word learning mean at your institution?
* Is it possible to define student learning Christianly?
* Is the meaning of the word learning at your institution grounded in a Christian view of life? Explain.
* What are the intended outcomes of student learning at your institution? What is your role in achieving them? others roles in achieving them? How successful are you at achieving them? How do you know?
* Is student learning enacted at your institution—both inside and outside of the classroom, both personally and structurally—in ways that reflect a Christian view of reality? Explain.
* Are all forms of learning held in the same regard at your institution?
* Are in-class and out-of-class learning initiatives complementary?
* Would you describe student learning at your institution as a coherent process?
* How would you describe the relationship among students, faculty, and staff in the learning process?
* Does your institution underscore the process nature of student learning? Does your student affairs division? If so, how?
* Is it appropriate to think of the purpose of student learning as wisdom development?
* What changes should be made, if any, to achieve greater consistency between institutional purpose and how student learning is achieved?

These are not idle questions for Christian student affairs professionals who claim an educational role within the institution. With slight modifications, they are easily adaptable to all types of institutions as well. If our argument is reasonable, the practices and activities associated with student affairs must correspond with the learning principles and outcomes that are established and valued by the institution. We also hope that the principles and purpose of student learning that we have offered will stir institutions and student affairs divisions—Christian and non-Christian alike—to reevaluate and perhaps reconsider their educational efforts.

Discerning Appropriate Contributions of Theory

An important point made in chapter 5 is that theories themselves are grounded in worldviews. A theory emerges from the questions that a theorist asks and is influenced by the assumptions that a theorist holds. To both understand theory and evaluate it, one must understand the context in which the theory was formed. To use theory, one needs to understand its formation so that the generalizability and applicability of theory to the present situation can be evaluated.

The grounds on which a Christian student affairs practitioner should critique developmental theory are its assumptions as well as its applications. A comparison should be made between the assumptions of a Christian worldview and the assumptions that underlie the theory that is being critiqued. In analyzing applications of the theory, one should consider whether the reality it says that it uncovers is reasonable; that is, does the reality explained seem to coincide with reality as he or she experiences and knows it based on a Christian point of view. The following questions may be instructive in evaluating the usefulness of a theory:

* What does this theory assume about the nature of persons? reality?
* What does the theory assume about the purpose of existence?
* What does this theory assume to be good? bad?
* What particular aspect of human development does this theory examine? Does the theory account for other aspects of persons? of development?
* What does the theory consider as the goal of human development? Is such a goal attainable? Are the theory's means for attaining such a goal reasonable?
* What is the context in which the theory was generated?
* What other assumptions may be reflected by the theory?

Perhaps it would be interesting for Christian student affairs practitioners to apply these questions to their own theories of young adult development and then to apply them to another theory of young adult development. A comparison of the responses may help to reveal the possible points of tension or contradiction between worldviews. The transcript of our discussion of

Chickering's theory is an example of such an idea and may, as such, be a useful guide in assisting Christian student affairs professionals in developing additional questions with which they can evaluate the nature and use of theory.

Considering Implications for Practice

In an effort to make this book as practical and helpful as possible for Christian student affairs professionals, chapter 6 included examples of programs that promote wisdom-focused student learning. Most of the examples illustrated efforts by thoughtful Christian practitioners to do student affairs differently, that is, to do student affairs through the filter of a Christian worldview. Our hope is that the inclusion of these examples will stimulate the examination of practices in Christian student affairs offices in particular. Insofar as each of the examples embody various principles of wisdom-focused student learning, however, we challenge student affairs divisions at other colleges to consider them as well, although we readily acknowledge that the particular content of such learning will be shaped differently.

As several of the examples in the chapter emphasized, knowing and doing are connected. In the context of student affairs, a relationship exists between our fundamental values and our practice of student affairs. Although we suggest that all practitioners consider this notion, we are particularly interested that Christian student affairs professionals intentionally and thoughtfully reflect on it as well. Several questions frame our interest:

* Does a relationship exist between Christian faith and the practice of student affairs? What is the nature of such a relationship?
* Do current student affairs practices reflect a commitment to wisdom-focused student learning based on a Christian point of view? Why or why not?
* How might the integrity of the relationship between Christian faith and wisdom-focused student learning initiatives viz-à-viz the student affairs profession be improved?

A Vision for the Future

The historical development of student affairs as presented in chapter 2 revealed the differing emphases and practices that have characterized the profession. The student development paradigm, which emerged after the 1960s, continues to enjoy considerable popularity among many practitioners. As we have already stated, we believe that many Christian student affairs professionals adopted the student development model without significant reflection. Perhaps these professionals have been too naive in assimilating contemporary professional standards without a corresponding effort to be discerning.

Not all Christian student affairs professionals, however, have accepted a student development model as the purpose and focus of their work. Some prefer what may be called a ministry model that, as the name suggests, emphasizes their framing their work as an extension of the church. In addition to fulfilling ordinary points of service such as housing, food, and activities this model apotheosizes Christian formation or discipleship as the overarching function of the profession. Professional preparation may include graduate work in a student affairs program, but training in biblical studies, theology, Christian education, and youth ministry is often considered more valuable. How these professionals define their helping students in Christian colleges become more Christlike may be considerably narrower compared to how we have attempted to define such a process.

We wonder if the tendency exists to assume that a ministry model of student affairs is *the* Christian approach to the profession or at least the most Christian approach. We urge caution in adopting such a viewpoint. As we have stated, student affairs exists with higher education, the fundamental context of which is student learning. A student affairs perspective, Christian or secular, must be developed with an understanding of and commitment to this context. The approach that we have taken in developing a Christian student affairs perspective is one that we believe may assist all administrators in Christian higher education in clarifying the Christian emphases of their colleges. Based on an understanding of its fundamental beliefs, a Christian college or university shapes an educational agenda. As a partner in the student learning project, student affairs must align itself with such an agenda. This process occurs most effectively as an ongoing dialog, particularly since personnel change over time. It is easy to forget that not everyone at an institution was present at its inception or at its critical moments; it is too frequently assumed that the fundamental values that provide meaning to the endeavor are known and understood by all.

We came together as a group of professionals with a concern regarding the direction of student affairs, particularly among our Christian colleagues. We began asking questions quickly and eagerly as we observed trends and discussions that baffled and disturbed us. Several of us remembered conversations and conference presentations in the 1980s that preceded and foreshadowed this book. Today, we are clearly not the only voices asking questions. For example, the paradigm of student development is undergoing critical scrutiny within the field itself. In concluding our comments, we thought that it would be valuable to examine two recent publications that are among the critical voices, with a particular view toward examining their implications for Christian student affairs professionals.

A recent monograph entitled *Reform in Student Affairs* (Bloland, Stamatakos, & Rogers, 1994) presents a concise overview of how and why student development became the operating premise of the profession. The authors critique the philosophy, theory, practice, and relevant research and literature of the student development movement and then offer the student affairs profession a new place to stand. Their new model suggests an educational agenda for student affairs that is grounded in the general education curriculum of an institution. Their argument is that the general education requirement is the best representation of what an institution perceives as essential knowledge. General education embodies the concept and nature of wholeness that an institution seeks to instill in its students. By aligning with the general education program, then, a student affairs division clearly identifies itself with the educational mission of the college and associates itself with the part of the curriculum that is designed to help students make connections within their college experience. In effect, the efforts of student affairs professionals may be considered part of students' general education.

Bloland, Stamatakos, and Rogers' critical review of the student development movement is very compelling. Likewise, their insistence that the student affairs profession "take its cue from the central educational mission of higher education" (1994, p. 103) (i.e., learning) is laudable. Notwithstanding many notable contributions in this work, we offer two observations. First, the authors seem eager to conflate "the central educational mission of higher education" and intellectual, or cognitive, development. Although we readily acknowledge that cognitive development is a vitally important and necessary part of student learning in college, we do not believe that student learning and cognitive development are interchangeable terms.

We also question the authors' aligning of the student affairs profession with general education. Our difficulty stems from the considerably less sanguine view we have of general education curricula. Theoretically, and in college catalogs, general education curricula reflect institutional commitments and provide coherence, yet breadth, to the undergraduate experience. In reality, however, the vast majority of general education curricula take shape around distribution requirements, which often provide little more than introductions to majors for nonmajors. Helping students establish connections is an afterthought if not unintentional altogether. Linking student affairs to general education, therefore, potentially sustains its marginality within the academy because it simply becomes one distinct part among many distinct parts within a college's general education program. In identifying learning with cognitive development and in associating the profession with general education curricula that are seldom more than the summative transcripts of disparate courses, Bloland, Stamatakos, and Rogers' new model for the student affairs profession may actually avoid what it seeks to harness—a unified, learning experience for college students.

Another critical voice, *The Student Learning Imperative*, was distributed at the 1994 American College Personnel Association's national conference. This terse document suggests that student affairs needs to modify its underlying purpose to focus on student learning and personal development, which it characterizes as synonymous concepts. Perhaps what is most helpful about this document is its charge to student affairs professionals to take learning seriously, which necessarily includes collaborating with others to fulfill intended learning outcomes effectively.

We identify two shortcomings of *The Student Learning Imperative*. First, although the statement readily concedes that "the concepts of 'learning,' 'personal development,' and 'student development' are inextricably intertwined and inseparable" (ACPA, 1994, p. 1), the document uses the phrase, "student learning and personal development," throughout. This creates confusion for the reader. The issue was further obfuscated at the 1995 annual meeting of the American College Personnel Association when the architects of the document, during a roundtable discussion on the statement, remained very unclear on precisely this point. One wonders whether those who composed the document really consider these concepts synonymous (which they say that they do); are predisposed to redundancy; or unconsciously differentiate between student learning, on the one hand, and personal development on the other. Whatever the case, we reiterate that we view student learning as the appropriate context of higher education and that students' personal development is a component part of the college learning experience.

We likewise wonder if the potential positive impact of this statement may be limited because some may interpret it as little more than an attempt to change the language that the student affairs profession uses to describe its purpose without changing what professionals actually do on their campuses. Student affairs has attempted to claim an educational, or learning, role within the academy for a number of years. The profession, however, has been sluggish in assessing learning that does occur, in documenting evidence that specific student affairs interventions produce specific identifiable learning outcomes, and in utilizing learning theory and principles to structure its role and activities. If the statement does, in fact, offer an old elixir in a new bottle without a concomitant interest in reframing the ways in which, and the purposes for which, the student affairs profession fulfills its roles, it will quickly become irrelevant.

We have suggested that the purpose of student learning is wisdom development, characterized by a value-shaped, purposeful, multidimensional, integrated, communal, ongoing process of remembering, discerning, and exploring. Perhaps to some readers, our voice many not seem unique. We are clearly not the first, nor will we be the last, to call American higher education to greater responsibility and accountability for student learning. *Involvement in Learning*, presented by the Study Group on the Conditions of Excellence in American Higher Education in 1984, was one of the early calls. A few years later, the work of Cross and Angelo (1988) in *Classroom Assessment Techniques* stressed that much of the focus in the classroom was on evaluating teaching rather than on improving student learning. Two years later Boyer (1990) lamented that for many faculty what was rewarded and therefore what was of importance was not teaching and student learning but rather research and publication. Recently, *An American Imperative: Higher Expectations for Higher Education* (1993) emphatically stressed the need for American higher education to put student learning first and to insist that learning be the central focus of the educational agenda.

Notwithstanding other voices past and present, we believe that we are proposing a unique, bold challenge to higher education. We are asking higher education, and all those who work within it, to reaffirm that student learning is for a purpose. Parker Palmer (1993, p. 69) writes that education is properly about creating spaces "where obedience to truth is practiced." He recognizes that learning and knowledge are not ends in themselves but rather means to particular ends; learning should be directed toward a purpose, a reason for the learning. Palmer calls for coupling responsibility with learning; our call for wisdom echoes his words. We are asking that the learning leadership of higher education join together in a conversation around vision and purpose, around shared expectations for students. There is danger in this conversation, however, if those who participate think not of students but of their own turf, and become preoccupied with protecting and maintaining what currently exists. Such has been too long the case. The dialog that we envision puts personal, departmental, and professional differences aside in favor of forging common ideals in community for the benefit of the students with whom we work. Such a discussion may lead to new models of learning leadership that effectively blur the lines between student affairs and academic affairs. Such a discussion may lead to the conferring of the title of educator on all persons who demonstrate that their efforts contribute to wisdom-focused student learning. Such a discussion may result in a redefinition of the curriculum to include all that occurs within the college context that shapes student learning as defined by the institution, regardless of whether the delivery site is a classroom, residence hall, concert, or coffee shop. Such a conversation may result in student affairs professionals being given faculty status not on an honorary basis but as an indication that their purpose and programs are crucial contributions to the learning project. Higher education may be at a point where it has an opportunity to change itself in significant ways. It is our hope that the ideas contained in this book will be one contribution in assisting Christian and non-Christian educators to pursue changes that reflect wisdom-focused student learning as the center of our enterprise.

References

American College Personnel Association (ACPA). (1994). *The student learning imperative: Implications for student affairs.* Alexandria, VA: ACPA.

Bloland, P., Stamatakos, L., & Rogers, R. (1994). *Reform in student affairs: A critique of student development.* Greensboro, NC: ERIC Counseling and Student Services Clearinghouse.

Boyer, E. (1990). *Scholarship reconsidered.* Princeton, NJ: Carnegie Foundation for the Advancement of Teaching.

Cross, K., & Angelo, T. (1988). *Classroom assessment technique: A handbook for faculty.* Ann Arbor, MI: National Center for Research on the Improvement of Postsecondary Teaching and Learning, University of Michigan.

Guthrie, D. (1994). Assessment as doxology. In D. Lee and G. Stronks (Eds.), *Assessment in Christian higher education: Rhetoric and reality* (pp. 221-232). Lanham, MD: University Press of America.

Palmer, P. (1993). *To know as we are known: Education as a spiritual journey.* San Francisco: HarperCollins

Study Group on the Conditions of Excellence in American Higher Education. (1984). *Involvement in learning.* Washington, DC: National Institute of Education.

Wingspread Group on Higher Education. (1993). *An American imperative: Higher expectations for higher education.* Racine, WI: The Johnson Foundation.

About the Contributors

Jay H. Barnes is the Provost of Bethel College (Minnesota), where his passion is to bring together programs in Academic Affairs, Student Life, and Campus Ministries to form a rich learning environment. He served for 15 years as Vice President for Student Development at Messiah College and as a past president of The Association for Christians in Student Development. He is a graduate of Wheaton College, University of Connecticut, and Loyola University - Chicago.

Jeanette Bult De Jong is the Vice President for Student Life at Calvin College and received her M.Ed. from the University of Toronto. She is presently the Chair of the Council of Chief Student Development Officers of the Coalition for Christian Colleges and Universities.

David S. Guthrie works at Calvin College as the Dean of Student Development, as an Adjunct Assistant Professor of Sociology, and as a Research Scholar in the Calvin Center for Christian Scholarship. He recently co-edited a monograph entitled *Agendas for Church-related Colleges and Universities*.

Kate Harrington has an Ed.D. from Harvard Graduate School of Education and has served as a faculty member and student affairs administrator at a number of institutions. She consults with higher education institutions and agencies on issues such as faculty roles and responsibilities, student populations and changing demographics, and organizational change.

Barry J. Loy is Dean of Students at Gordon College and is a graduate of the University of North Carolina at Chapel Hill and Wheaton College (IL). He is presently the Treasurer and Membership Chair of the Association for Christians in Student Development.

William M. Painter is the Vice President for Ministry with the Coalition for Christian Outreach. For more than twenty years he has placed, trained, and managed people in the fields of campus ministry and student development.

Miriam Sailers Ed.D., has a doctorate from the University of Toronto, Ontario, Canada. She began her career in higher education as a student government officer and Resident Advisor while in college. She has since served in such various student affairs roles as Director of Residence Life, Associate Dean of Students, and Dean of Students. Her primary interest is in helping students make connections between what they learn, what they believe, and how they live.

D. Terry Thomas holds a dual appointment as Assistant Professor of Biblical studies and Education at Geneva College in Beaver Falls, PA. He is the Director of the college's Master of Arts in Higher Education program and has worked with the Pittsburgh Coalition for Christian Outreach for twenty-five years.

Made in the USA
San Bernardino, CA
21 August 2015